WHAT REALLY HAPPENED?

JFK

WHAT REALLY HAPPENED?

JFK

Five Hundred and One Questions and Answers

By Joan Hubbard-Burrell

Ponderosa Press
Spring Branch, Texas

Published by Ponderosa Press
P.O. Box 192
Spring Branch, Texas 78070

Cover photograph by Douglass H. Hubbard

Cover design by Margie Montreuil

Printed in the United States of America

First Edition

Library of Congress Catalog Card #92-062333

ISBN Number: 0-9634795-9-8

This book is dedicated with love to my husband Jim and our two special children, Jason & Lara . . .but especially to my parents, Doug & Fran Hubbard for their constant love, encouragement and support.

Acknowledgements:

Special thanks to:

My parents for hours spent brainstorming and editing, to Larry Howard and Robert Johnson of the JFK Assassination Information Center for giving me access to their archives, and to Carolyn DeFever for all the good advice.

JHB

Contents

Foreword

Twenty-nine years have passed since the assassination of President John F. Kennedy. His death on November 22, 1963 changed the history of the world. Oliver Stone said it best when he labeled his film "JFK" as "The Story That Won't Go Away."

With all of the latest controversy since the movie "JFK" and the possibility of the Warren Commission and the House Select Committee files being released in the near future, many more questions are being asked. As Director and President of the JFK Assassination Information Center, along with Robert T. Johnson, the Director of Archives, we are able to answer only a small percentage of these questions due to the limited time we can spend with each individual.

I am proud to have been asked to write the foreword for this book -- *What Really Happened? JFK - 501 Questions and Answers.* Not only is the book fascinating and intriguing to read, but it also helps the reader understand the cast of characters involved in the murder of the century. Without knowing the characters, it is virtually impossible to unravel this mystery, as I have learned through my ten years of investigation. Whenever possible, pictures are provided to accompany the text, thus enabling one to relate visually to each character.

I applaud this tremendous undertaking by Joan Hubbard-Burrell. This book is a must-read and a very important addition to anyone's personal collection of assassination books. I must say it would have made my job easier with Oliver Stone in the making of the movie "JFK" if I had had this book with me as a research guide on the set during the eighty-five days of filming. Read and enjoy.

"The truth shall prevail."

Larry N. Howard

Preface:

One of the most complex mysteries in our history is the untimely death of President John F. Kennedy on 22 November 1963. Thirty years after his death we still don't know *what really happened.*

The answers to the 501 questions which follow are not mine. Rather, they have been gleaned from the books cited on the following pages.

Almost all are of recent publication and should be readily available to the reader wishing to pursue this mystery in greater depth.

To these authors and their publishers I give sincere thanks. To you, my readers, I hope you find some answers.

JHB

Key to Footnotes:

AOT - *Act of Treason* by Mark North, Carroll & Graf Publishers, Inc., New York, N.Y.

BE - *Best Evidence* by David Lifton , Carroll & Graf Publishers, Inc., New York, N.Y.

C - *Conspiracy* by Anthony Summers, Paragon House, New York, N.Y.

COA - *Contract on America* by David Scheim, Kensington Publishing Corp., New York, N.Y.

CF - *Crossfire* by Jim Marrs, Carroll & Graf Publishers, Inc., New York, N.Y.

DP - *Death Of A President* by William Manchester, Harper & Row Publishers, Inc., New York

DC - *Double Cross* by Sam & Chuck Giancana, Warner Books, Inc., New York, N.Y.

FH - *Fatal Hour* by G. Robert Blakey & Richard N. Billings, Berkley Books, New York, N.Y.

HT - *High Treason* by Robert Groden & Harrison Livingstone, The Berkley Publishing Group, New York, N.Y.

HTII - *High Treason 2* by Harrison Livingstone, Carroll & Graf Publishers, Inc. N. Y., N.Y.

K - *The Kennedys, An American Drama* by Peter Collier & David Horowitz, Warner Books Inc., New York, N.Y

MK - *Mafia Kingfish* by John Davis, NAL Penguin, Inc., New York, N.Y.

OTT - *On The Trail Of The Assassins* by Jim Garrison, Sheridan Square Press, New York, N.Y.

PL - *Peter Lawford, The Man Who Kept The Secrets* by James Spada, Bantam Books, New York, N.Y.

PA - *Presidential Anecdotes* by Paul F. Boller, Jr., Penguin Books, USA Inc., New York, N.Y.

PD - *Plausible Denial* by Mark Lane, Thunder's Mouth Press, New York, N.Y.

PP - *Presidential Passions* by Michael Sullivan, Shapolsky Publishers, Inc., New York, N.Y.

RC - *The Ruby Cover-up* by Seth Kantor, Zebra Books, Kensington Publishing Company, New York, N.Y.

RD - *Reasonable Doubt* by Henry Hurt, Henry Holt & Company, Inc., New York, N.Y.

RTJ - *Rush to Judgement* by Mark Lane, Thunder's Mouth Press, New York N.Y.

SS - *Spy Saga* by Philip H. Melanson, Praeger Publishers, New York, N.Y.

TC - *The Texas Connection* by Craig I. Zirbel, The Texas Connection Company, Scottsdale, Arizona

* Indicates description of person can be found in the Cast of Characters section beginning on page 58.

Setting The Scene: Dallas

Here is a list of the miscellaneous "errors in judgement" which contributed to the disaster on 22 November 1963.

1. The Mayor of Dallas in November 1963 was Earle Cabell. Responsibility for motorcade security was his.

2. The Mayor's brother, General Charles Cabell had returned to Dallas after being fired from the CIA by JFK following the Bay of Pigs disaster.

3. JFK had threatened to cancel the oil depletion allowance which had helped oil people accumulate huge fortunes.

4. The motorcade route was changed the morning of the assassination. Originally it was to proceed straight down Main Street and not make the sharp turns onto Houston & Elm.

5. When President Kennedy visited Yosemite National Park in August of 1962 children of Park employees who had climbed trees for a better view of the President were ordered down by the Secret Service, yet open windows along the motorcade route were not secured.

6. The motorcade was travelling too slowly and it was against all Secret Service regulations to make the 120 degree turn from Houston Street onto Elm Street.

7. The limousine was to have been eighth in the motorcade followed by the press bus. Instead, it was second and the press bus was in the rear.

8. The 112th Military Intelligence Unit on alert at Fort Sam Houston in San Antonio was told it would not be needed for security that morning.

9. Dallas Sheriff's deputies were ordered not to take part in security.

10. The President's Secret Service detail was out carousing until the early morning hours of the 22nd. Only one agent on the follow-up car responded when the shots were first heard. He was ordered back.

11. The agent driving the limousine put his foot on the brakes when the first shot was fired and didn't accelerate until after the fatal shot.

12. A police radio channel jammed and the phone in the press bus went dead.

13. Although Mrs. Kennedy and the Secret Service wanted the bubble-top installed on the limousine, the President did not. Mrs. Kennedy was a political asset and he wanted the people of Dallas to be able to see her.

14. If the luncheon had been held at the Women's Building in Fair Park (the site preferred by the Secret Service for security reasons), instead of the Trade Mart, the motorcade would have been two blocks away from the Texas School Book Depository and travelling at a greater rate of speed.

Who Was Lee Harvey Oswald?

A Profile:

In the years since the assassination of President Kennedy a different picture of Lee Harvey Oswald has emerged. Originally we were led to believe that he was a lonely, confused, left-wing misfit as well as a school drop-out.

Actually, he was very intelligent. While in the Marine Corps he became fluent in Russian and reportedly was fluent in Spanish as well. He enjoyed reading and read 27 books in the summer of 1963 including some about President Kennedy.

From the time he entered the Marine Corps until his death, his life was a mystery. We have learned that he was highly-trained in the intelligence field and he apparently believed his work in intelligence was for the purpose of serving his country.

We know he was a loving father and it is my hope that the investigations will continue and that, for the sake of his children, he will someday be vindicated.

JHB

The Story Begins

Q. How did John F. Kennedy win the election?

A. There were voting discrepancies in Chicago in the 1960 Presidential election. Had it not been for ballot-box-stuffing in Cook County, the state of Illinois would have gone Republican. Mayor Richard Daley's forces blocked the recount request and was reinforced by Sam Giancana*, Mafia boss.

CF - Page 175
DC - Page 279, 281, 289, 290

Q. What were President Kennedy's feelings about the war in Vietnam?

A. He felt the Vietnamese people needed to be doing more for themselves. He said "in the final analysis its their war, they're the ones to have to win it or lose it." He had started withdrawing American troops and planned to bring all American personnel home within the next two years.

C - Page 396
HT - Page 423

Q. Who was really in control of the Vietnam war?

A. Fletcher Prouty* said the combat phase was under the control and direction of the CIA.

HT - Page 444
OTT - Page 177

Q. What was National Security Action Memoranda (NSAM) 273?

A. It reversed President Kennedy's policy to withdraw American troops from Vietnam. It was signed four days after the assassination and from that date on the war quickly escalated.

PD - Page 107

Q. Was the Bay of Pigs invasion deliberately sabotaged?

A. Fletcher Prouty reportedly said it was sabotaged to embarrass President Kennedy.

HT - Page 434

Q. How was Fletcher Prouty involved with the Bay of Pigs invasion?

A. He was responsible for finding two United States Naval crafts capable of carrying tanks, men, ammunition and weapons.

PD - Page 332

Q. Was George Bush involved with the Bay of Pigs invasion?

A. According to author Mark Lane the actual name for the invasion was "Operation Zapata" -- George Bush's oil company's name is Zapata Petroleum Midland. The names given to the two ships obtained by Fletcher Prouty were "Barbara" and "Houston".

PD - Page 332

Q. What was the primary cause for the Cuban Missile Crisis?

A. The United States had placed intercontinental ballistic missiles in Turkey. The missiles were aimed at the Soviet Union.

HTII - Page 26

Q. Did President Kennedy try to control the power of members of the CIA and military in the Pentagon?

A. Yes. After the Bay of Pigs fiasco he signed National Security Action Memoranda #55 which placed responsibility for peacetime activity with the Chairman of the Joint Chiefs of Staff.

CF - Page 304

Q. What was Operation MONGOOSE?

A. It was the name given to the CIA plots to assassinate Fidel Castro. This fact is well-documented and the plotting continued well after President Kennedy ordered them to stop.

CF - Beginning Page 400

Q. What was Alpha 66?

A. It was an anti-Castro group whose leader was "violently anti-Kennedy". The group reportedly was in Dallas at the time of the assassination.

SS - Page 111

Q. How did President Kennedy feel about Fidel Castro?

A. He approved of the Cuban revolution but did not like having a Communist threat so close to the U.S. He was secretly working toward resuming diplomatic relations with Cuba. In fact, an American envoy was with Castro at the time the President was killed.

C - Beginning Page 398
FH - Page 66

Q. What was Castro's opinion of JFK?

A. He said, "He still has the possibility of becoming, in the eyes of history, the greatest President of the United States, the leader who may at last understand that there can be co-existence between capitalists and socialists, even in the Americas". He also said he would be willing to say he was a friend of Goldwater if it would help get JFK re-elected.

C - Pages 406 & 407
PD - Page 107

Q. Did the CIA ever compile a psychological profile of President Kennedy?

A. Yes, according to Jim Garrison* one was compiled shortly after his election. One of its purposes was to predict positions he might take if certain conditions arose.

OTT - Page 60

Q. Did President Kennedy plan to dissolve the CIA?

A. Yes. According to author Mark Lane, he planned to replace the CIA with an intelligence organization that would be loyal to the President.

RTJ - Page viii

Q. What was ARTICHOKE?

A. It was the CIA's behavior-modification program staffed by a hypnotist, a technician, a drug expert and a psychiatrist.

CF - Page 185

Q. What was MK/ULTRA?

A. It was the name given to the CIA's drug studies. In 1953 the Agency reportedly purchased LSD at a cost of $240,000. After experimenting they determined it would not accomplish their objective of mind-altering and information gathering.

CF - Page 185
RD - Page 303

Q. What was ZR/RIFLE?

A. It was a CIA code name for the Agency's program for committing foreign assassinations.

CF - Page 205
FH - Page 59

30

Q. What did former CIA Director George Bush reportedly say about the Agency?

A. According to a UPI report George Bush "admitted the CIA had been guilty of abuse of power, but defended the need for an intelligence-gathering agency, covert operations and spying in other countries."

HT - Page 355

Q. Did the CIA and FBI have offices in New Orleans?

A. Yes. According to Jim Garrison they were both located in the Masonic Temple in the 300 block of Saint Charles Avenue.

OTT - Page 27

Q. What did Fletcher Prouty say about clandestine operations?

A. "The paramount condition underlying any approval for clandestine operations is absolute control at the top."

HT - Page 425

Q. Were there other plans to assassinate JFK?

A. Yes. There were at least three in the fall of 1963. The information was withheld from the Secret Service agent responsible for the President's protection and from the Dallas office of the Service.

CF - Page 242

Q. Had there been other threats on President Kennedy's life?

A. Yes, several. In September of 1962 Mafia boss Santos Trafficante* reportedly said "Kennedy's not going to make it to the election. He is going to be hit."

New Orleans Mafia boss Carlos Marcello* was also said to have threatened JFK and referring to Robert Kennedy, we are told he said "He's going to be taken care of. The dog will keep biting you if you only cut off its tail".

Prior to President Kennedy's scheduled visit to Chicago on November 2 the Secret Service heard of a threat and the trip was cancelled.

The President was also scheduled to visit Miami on November 18. Joseph Milteer's threat had been reported so the planned motorcade was cancelled and he was flown by helicopter.

Reportedly there were over 400 threats on the President's life between March and November of 1963.

C - Pages 254, 258, 403, 405
DC - Page 333
FH - Page 7
MK
OTT - Page 181

Q. Did FBI Director Hoover* have prior knowledge of the Presidential assassination?

A. Yes. He had developed an intelligence system during his 30 years with the FBI. Author James Hepburn said "the Dallas conspiracy was born and took root in places where the FBI was well represented. By mid-October, Hoover had been informed of the existence of a plot and was familiar with many of the details. The week before the President's departure for Texas, Hoover knew exactly what was going to happen."

AOT
HT - Page 309

Q. What did the FBI do with this information?

A. Apparently they did not pass the information on to the Secret Service. In the cases of the Chicago and Miami plots apparently the Secret Service failed to inform their own agents who were responsible for planning the Dallas trip.

C - Pages 255, 259, 405

Q. Did the FBI office in Philadelphia record any Mafia death threat against the President?

A. Yes. On 9 September 1962 a conversation between underworld figures Angelo Bruno and William Weisburg in which Weisburg threatened the President was recorded and sent to Hoover who did not inform the Attorney General or the Secret Service.

AOT - Page 128
FH - Page 270

Q. Did any FBI employee receive a TELEX message warning of the assassination?

A. Yes, William Walter working in the New Orlean's office of the Bureau received a teletype on 17 November 1963 warning of a threat to kill the President in Dallas on 22 November. Walter said he immediately informed the five agents who would have been responsible for investigating such a threat. Walter copied the TELEX word-for-word before filing it. The original message disappeared from the file after the assassination.

OTT - Page 220

Q. What does the FBI Handbook say about threats to the President?

A. "Any information indicating the possibility of an attempt against the person or safety of the President, members of the immediate family of the President, President-elect or Vice-President must be referred immediately by the most expeditious means of communication to the nearest office of the United States Secret Service."

AOT - Page 41

Q. Did Oswald have ties to the FBI?

A. Yes. According to many researchers and an FBI memorandum dated 16 March 1964 (Soviet Section).

CF - Page 472
FBI Memorandum

Q. Did the FBI contact Marina Oswald prior to the assassination?

A. Yes. According to Marina Oswald and her friend Ruth Paine* they were visited more than once by FBI Agent James Hosty in the last two weeks of Lee's life.

C - Page 369
FH - Page 39

Q. Did FBI Agent James Hosty threaten Marina Oswald with deportation?

A. According to Oswald on two occasions Agent Hosty threatened Marina with having to return to Russia.

CF - Page 235

Q. Did JFK ever talk about the possibility of an assassination?

A. Yes, in Fort Worth on the morning of November 22 in comments to Mrs. Kennedy and to aide Kenneth O'Donnell.

C - Page 2
DP - Page 121
FH - Page 5

Q. Was the President wearing his back brace?

A. Yes. It has been documented that he could barely stand without his back brace which he wrapped tightly with ace-bandages. This may be the reason he did not fall over when initially struck.

DP - Page 183

Q. Was there a problem choosing the luncheon site in Dallas?

A. Yes. Because it was more secure, the Secret Service preferred the Women's Building in Fair Park. The Trade Mart, more modern and more acceptable to citizens of Dallas, was selected instead. If it had been held at the Women's

Building, the motorcade would not have been near the Texas School Book Depository and would have been moving faster.

CF - Page 243
FH - Pages 3 & 6

Q. Was the motorcade route changed?

A. Yes, on the morning of 22 November 1963. Originally it was to proceed straight down Main and not turn onto Houston & Elm. If the route had not been changed the motorcade would not have been moving so slowly nor have been so close to the Texas School Book Depository and the Grassy Knoll.

FH - Page 6
OTT - Pages 101-103

Q. What is "Presidential Protection"?

A. Certain military personnel are trained to assist the Secret Service in protecting the President when needed.

PD - xv

Q. What was wrong with "Presidential Protection" on 22 November 1963?

A. The 112th Military Intelligence Group, stationed at Fort Sam Houston, poised to leave for Dallas, was told to stand down and not report for duty.

CF - Page 309
HT - Page 352
PD - Page xv

Q. Where was the President's Secret Service detail on the night before the assassination?

A. Reportedly, nine of them went out for drinks at the Cellar Club (while still on duty) leaving two Fort Worth firemen to guard the President. At 2:00 a.m. seven were still drinking, most of them continued to do so until 3:00 a.m. They were not disciplined for their actions. An interesting historical footnote: President Lincoln was assassinated when his bodyguard went next door for a drink.

CF - Pages 246-247
HT - Pages 15, 149-150

Q. Were any of Vice President Johnson's Secret Service agents out with the President's detail the night before the assassination?

A. No.

CF - Page 249

Q. How fast was the motorcade travelling as it neared the assassination point?

A. They were moving at about eleven miles per hour when they turned onto Elm Street. Secret Service regulations state that the Presidential limousine is to proceed "at a good speed" and to not take unnecessary or hazardous routes which would slow it down. The manual says the car is to move at 44 miles per hour.

HT - Page 156

Q. Did the sniper have a clear view of the motorcade from the sixth floor of the Texas School Book Depository?

A. Not when the first round was fired. The view was obstructed by a large tree.

OTT - Page 99

Q. How did the President's Secret Service detail respond when the shots were fired?

A. Riding in the car directly behind the President's they remained motionless. Secret Service Agent Emory Roberts ordered them not to move after the first shot. Had prompt action been taken the President might have been saved.

CF - Pages 15 & 245
HT - Pages 16, 148 & 149
RD - Page 14

Q. Did any Secret Service agent (besides Clint Hill) react when the shooting began?

A. Yes, John Ready jumped off the running-board of the follow-up car but he was ordered back by Special Agent-in-Charge Emory Roberts.

CF - Page 249

Q. Did the Secret Service agent driving the limousine accelerate after the first shot was fired?

A. No. Approximately 5.6 seconds elapsed between the first and the last shot fired. A motion picture indicates that the agent kept his foot on the brakes during the shooting and until the fatal shots were fired.

C - Page 3
CF - Page 12
HT - Pages 22 & 149

Q. Did the Secret Service follow-up car almost hit the limousine?

A. Yes. When the initial shots were fired the Secret Service follow-up car almost hit the rear bumper.

CF - Page 245

Q. What did Presidential Aide Kenneth O'Donnell write years later?

A. "If the Secret Service agents had acted more quickly and if the driver of the Presidential limousine had hit the gas instead of the brake, might President Kennedy's life have been spared?"

CF - Page 248

Q. Was the President protected as well as he should have been?

A. No. The findings of the Assassinations Committee were that security precautions were "uniquely insecure" on 22 November 1963.

HT - Page 155

Q. Who was responsible for most of the security precautions?

A. Secret Service Agent Winston Lawson.

HT - Page 155

Q. Did JFK's limousine have fewer motorcycle outriders than usual in Dallas?

A. Yes. Chief of Police Curry wanted eight officers to flank the Presidential car, but Secret Service Agent Winston Lawson ordered the number reduced to four to ride near the rear fenders instead of at the sides.

CF - Page 244

Q. Why was Jacqueline Kennedy climbing out onto the trunk of the limousine?

A. According to authors Robert Groden and Harrison Livingstone she was trying to retrieve part of the President's skull.

HT - Page 230

Q. What did Secret Service Agent Paul Landis report?

A. Landis, riding in the car behind the President, stated that the fatal shot came from in front of the President's car.

However, he was not called to testify before the Warren Commission.

C - Page 24
CF - Page 14
RTJ - Page 42

Q. Was there a problem with the telephone system in Washington D.C. on the afternoon of the assassination?

A. Sources have reported that twenty-five seconds after the last bullet was fired the telephone system in Washington went dead and it took one hour for service to be restored.

DP - Page 193
HT - Page 19

Q. What happened to the telephone in the motorcade press bus?

A. It has been reported that the press telephone was immobilized at 12:34. One reporter was able to get out word of the shooting before the system went down.

HT - Page 20

Q. Were there problems with police radio channels?

A. It has been documented that at 12:29 Dallas Police radio Channel One went dead, and for four minutes someone blocked the channel by keeping his microphone open.

FH - Page 14
HT - Page 20

Q. Was a morse code signal heard over the Dallas Police radio?

A. Sheriff Jim Bowles of Dallas told author Livingstone that moments after the fatal shot was fired the Morse code signal "V" (for "victory") was heard over the police radio.

HT - Pages 126 & 248

Q. In the confusion following the shooting was there one place that attracted the most attention?

A. Yes, the Grassy Knoll.

C - Pages 49 & 50
CF - Page 14

Q. Did anyone see smoke in the trees on the Grassy Knoll?

A. A group of witnesses on the Triple Underpass heard a bang and saw a puff of smoke coming from in front of the fence on the Grassy Knoll.

CF - Page 58

Q. Did Lee Bowers, working in the railroad control tower behind the Grassy Knoll, see anything unusual?

A. Yes. He saw two men behind the fence, cars driving through the area, and a puff of smoke during the shooting.

C - Page 28
CF - Page 75
FH - Page 101

HT - Page 134

Q. Were footprints found in the mud behind the fence on the Grassy Knoll?

A. Yes, a Union Terminal car inspector named James Simmons stated that he and Dallas Patrolman Foster ran behind the fence as soon as they heard the shots. There they found footprints in the mud as well as on the 2x4 fence railing.

CF - Page 58

Q. What did Secret Service Agent Forrest Sorrels report?

A. While riding in the lead car, he said that sounds of shots seemed to come from the direction of the Grassy Knoll. He later changed his testimony.

C - Page 23
RTJ - Page 42

Q. How many people in or near the Texas School Book Depository stated that shooting came from the Grassy Knoll?

A. Sixteen.

C - Page 23

Q. Did any police officers think the shots came from the Grassy Knoll?

A. Yes. In fact Dallas County Sheriff Bill Decker, riding in the car in front of the President, ordered all available men from his department into the railroad yards behind the knoll.

C - Page 24
CF - Page 14

Q. Was a bullet found on the south side of Elm Street?

A. Yes. Several witnesses, including a police officer, reported seeing a bullet hit the grass near a manhole cover on the south side of Elm Street. The bullet, reportedly pocketed by an FBI Agent, was never seen again.

CF - Page 315
HT - Page 214

Q. Were other bullets and shell casings found?

A. Yes. A fragment identified as 6.5 millimeter ammunition was found on the south side of Dealey Plaza. A Stemmons

Freeway sign which momentarily blocked the view of the motorcade on the Zapruder film was reportedly struck by a bullet but does not appear in photographs taken the day after the assassination. A 30.06 shell casing which possibly held a 6.5mm sabot bullet, was found 12 years later on the top of the Dallas County Records Building giving rise to the theory that it might have held a bullet first fired from the "Oswald" rifle.

CF - Page 317

Q. What is a "sabot"?

A. A sabot is a plastic sleeve that allows a larger caliber weapon to fire a smaller caliber slug. According to Dean Morgan, his father, while repairing air-conditioning equipment on the roof of the Dallas County Records Building in 1975, found a fired 30.06 caliber shell casing. It had a neck-crimp consistent with the use of a sabot. This suggests that the assassins could have fired at the President with a high-powered rifle using bullets which had previously been fired from Oswald's rifle.

CF - Page 317

Q. Did anyone think the President had been shot by a high-powered rifle?

A. Yes, the doctors at Parkland Hospital and witnesses in Dealey Plaza.

CF - Page 12
HT - Page 214

Q. What did Police Chief Jesse Curry do as soon as the shots were fired?

A. He ordered that an officer get up onto the Triple Underpass. Later he reportedly said that he could tell that the shots originated near the Book Depository.

RTJ - Page 43

Q. Did any eye-witness hear more than three gunshots?

A. Yes, Maurice Orr, who stood on the side closest to the car and closest to the President thinks there could have been as many as five shots. Witness Jean Hill said she heard four to six shots (not echoes) and sounds of different guns being fired.

Carolyn Walther heard four shots fired and A.J. Millican heard eight.

C - Page 20
CF - Pages 21 & 29

Q. Did anyone hear two shots close together?

A. Yes. Secret Service Agent Kellerman described the last sound as a "double-bang". Agent Greer, the driver, said the last shot cracked out "just behind" its predecessor.

C - Page 19

Q. Did any witnesses hear shooting from the Dal-Tex building?

A. According to Jim Garrison witnesses heard gunfire from both the Texas School Book Depository and the Dal-Tex building. A man who came running out of the Dal-Tex building was arrested but later released. Apparently the Sheriff's office did not even record his name. Jim Braden* was also arrested and released.

HT - Page 121
OTT - Page 205

Q. Did any of the gunshots miss?

A. Yes, the first one struck pavement in the middle of the south-most lane on Elm Street just behind the President's limousine.

CF - Pages 14 & 27

Q. Did any witnesses claim to have smelled gunpowder in the air?

A. Yes, including three riders in the motorcade.

C - Page 29
CF - Page 16

Q. What was Senator Ralph Yarborough's comment regarding gunpowder?

A. Riding in the third vehicle in the motorcade, Yarborough has stated that he could smell gunpowder in the car almost all the way to Parkland Hospital. He was not called to testify before the Warren Commission.

HT - Page 16
RTJ - Page 44

Q. Was there a recording of gunshots in Dealey Plaza?

A. Yes. The acoustic evidence was found on a "dictabelt" recording of police radio traffic made on 22 November proving there was more than one gunman.

C - Page 14
HT - Pages 7 & 220

Q. What did the acoustic scientist's report show?

A. All but the third shot originated in the vicinity of the sixth floor southeast corner of the Texas School Book Depository, and that shots could have come from the nearby Dal Tex building. Shot #3 came from the Grassy Knoll.

54

C - Page 21
FH - Page 114

Q. Did the FBI examine the Dictabelt recordings?

A. According to authors Groden and Livingstone in review-
ing the findings of the Assassinations Committee the FBI
ignored all recordings entirely.

HT - Page 255

Q. Did recorded gunshots match the Zapruder film?

A. Yes. Unfortunately only the Texas School Book
Depository and Grassy Knoll were tested while the sixteen
other possible locations were not. It is believed that if they
had been tested there would have been a probable result of
"six or more shots fired from at least three locations".

HT - Page 261

Q. What did Robert Blakey, Chief Counsel for the Assassinations Committee say about the comparison of the tape and film?

A. Author Robert Groden has stated he was instructed by Blakey not to reveal to the Assassinations Committee any conclusions he had come to regarding the tapes and the film.

HT - Page 262

Q. Did anyone hear revolver shots?

A. Secret Service agents present testified that they thought they heard a revolver being fired. Some researchers believe that a revolver was fired from the sewer next to the limousine.

HT - Page 215

Q. Did anyone find a .45 caliber slug in Dealey Plaza?

A. Yes, Deputy Sheriff Buddy Walthers found one on the south side of Elm Street.

HT - Page 214

Q. What is "triangulation of crossfire"?

A. According to David Ferrie* it meant shooting at the President from three directions.

OTT - Page 154

Q. Was there a "barrage" of gunshots in Dealey Plaza?

A. According to eyewitnesses and acoustical evidence a fusillade of shots came from at least three directions and perhaps more.

HT - Page 264

Q. Is there evidence that shots were fired from the Triple Underpass?

A. Yes. According to authors Groden and Livingstone a bullet mark on the sidewalk in Dealey Plaza pointed directly to a "manhole on the overpass" which would have been a perfect sniper's nest. The manhole has since been paved over.

HT - Page 118

Q. What were the angles of the bullets?

A. It was reported that the bullet which struck Governor Connally entered at a twenty-five degree downward angle. The President was hit by a bullet which entered at a forty-five to sixty degree downward angle.

HT - Page 265

Q. How many bullets hit the President from the front?

A. According to researchers at least two. One struck him in the throat and the other hit him in the head.

HT - Page 265

Q. What kind of bullet caused the President's head wound?

A. According to Groden and Livingstone it was caused by either a hand gun or a hunting style bullet, not by the "military jacketed" bullet like the one found on the stretcher at Parkland Hospital. They report that a military jacketed bullet seldom fragments upon impact which the one that struck the President did.

HT - Page 264

Q. Was there damage to the President's chest?

A. According to Dr. Marion Jenkins who was present in the emergency room at Parkland Hospital "there was also obvious chest damage" and the surgeons inserted drainage tubes.

HT - Page 64

Q. How did Dr. McClelland describe the President's cause of death?

A. A "massive head and brain injury from a gunshot wound of the left temple". He later changed his statement to a "massive head and brain injury from a gunshot wound of the right rear occipital area." (Per Larry Howard).

HT - Page 37
OTT - Page 92

Q. Was the Texas School Book Depository searched thoroughly?

A. According to author Henry Hurt the "Oswald rifle" was found less than one hour after the shooting and apparently after its discovery the search of the building and its contents ended.

RD - Page 386

Q. Was there anything unusual about the ammunition found in the Texas School Book Depository?

A. The manufacturer stated it was no longer being produced commercially by them. They also said "the reliability of such ammunition would be questionable today". The Warren Commission reported that the ammunition had been "recently made".

CF - Page 201
RTJ - Page 122

Q. Did anyone think the empty cartridges found on the sixth floor of the Texas School Book Depository had been planted.

A. Yes, Jim Garrison questioned their authenticity because of their "neat distribution pattern". Normally a rifle cartridge is flung away when the weapon is fired.

OTT - Page 98

Q. Was the rifle found in the Texas School Book Depository first identified as a bolt-action Mauser instead of a Mannlicher-Carcano carbine?

A. Deputy Constable Seymour Weitzman who owned gunshops identified it as a Mauser.

HT - Pages 5, 73, 229, 232
OTT - Page 98
RD - Page 102
RTJ - Page 114

Q. What was unusual about the ammunition for the Mannlicher-Carcano found in the Texas School Book Depository?

A. It was from a lot manufactured by Western Cartridge Corporation in the mid-1950's on a U.S. Government contract.

CF - Page 201

Q. How did Mechanix Illustrated describe the Mannlicher Carcano?

A. "Crudely made, poorly designed, dangerous and inaccurate".

RTJ - Page 123

Q. What did author Jack O'Connor write about the Mannlicher-Carcano?

A. He said it has a "coy habit of blowing the firing pin out in the shooter's face".

RTJ - Page 123

Q. Could the rifle found in the Depository have been aimed and fired twice in 1.66 seconds -- the gap between shots 1 and 2?

A. No. The firing times for two shots by the FBI's best marksmen were 2.23 and 2.25 seconds.

C - Page 46

Q. What were the results of the rifle tests arranged by the Warren Commission?

A. Three riflemen rated as Master by the National Rifle Association were unable to shoot as fast as the so-called assassin and none of them was able to strike the enlarged head or neck on their stationary target even once, even though shims had been added to their sights to improve accuracy. Oswald was supposed to have struck a moving target twice and he was known to have been a poor shot.

RTJ - Pages 126-127

Q. What is a "shim"?

A. Webster's describes it as "a thin often tapered piece of wood, metal, or stone used (as in leveling something) to fill in".

Q. What rifles did former CIA operative Robert Morrow purchase?

A. He said that he bought four Mannlicher-Carcano rifles on instructions from the CIA. He believed that at least one of the four ended up in the hands of the Dallas police.

CF - Page 201

Q. Was the rifle found in the Texas School Book Depository examined for fingerprints?

A. Yes, none were found in Dallas. The rifle was then flown to FBI headquarters in Washington, D.C. The traces found there were not complete enough to identify. Four days later a palm print said to have been "lifted" from the barrel in Dallas was sent to the FBI by the Dallas police and was identified as Lee Harvey Oswald's. He reportedly was fingerprinted after he was in his casket.

C - Page 56
HT - Page 170
RD - Page 106

Q. Was any film seized by the FBI in Dealey Plaza?

A. Yes. Eyewitness Beverly Oliver, also known as the "Babushka Lady", says her 8mm film was seized by someone she believed to be FBI agent Regis Kennedy. She never saw it again.

HT - Page 121

Q. What message was sent to President Johnson aboard Air Force One on the afternoon of the assassination?

A. Reportedly the White House Situation Room sent a message stating there was no conspiracy and only one person committed the crime.

HT - Page 20

Q. Where were the members of the Cabinet at the time of the assassination?

A. The following Cabinet members and Presidential aides were on a plane enroute to Japan: Secretary of the Treasury C. Douglas Dillon, Secretary of Agriculture Orville Freeman, Secretary of the Interior Stewart Udall, Secretary of Labor Willard Wirtz, Secretary of State Dean Rusk, Secretary of Commerce Luther Hodges, Walter Heller, Chairman of the President's Council of Economic Advisors, Press Secretary Pierre Salinger, Assistant Secretary of State Robert Manning and White House staff member Mike Feldman.

DP - Page 193
FH - Page 18

Q. When they heard about the shooting in Dallas were they able to communicate with the White House?

A. No, because the official code book was missing from its normal place on the plane. They could not send messages without it.

HT - Page 20

Cast of Characters

These people all played a part in this mystery and are all pieces
of the puzzle which I hope will fall into place later.

Q. Who was James Angleton?

A. He was CIA Chief of Counter Intelligence who rehearsed
with William Sullivan the questions and answers they would
give Warren Commission investigators. He was described by
author Anthony Summers as "a master of deception and dis-
information."

C - Page 112
FH - Page 88
HT - Page 333
HTII - Page 377
MK - Page 296
PD - Page 143
SS - Page 131

Q. Who was Sergio Archaca-Smith?

A. He was an anti-Castro exile involved with Guy Banister in New Orleans and the New Orleans representative of the Cuban Revolutionary Council. He reportedly said he was "controlled by the CIA". He had moved to Texas by 1963. When Jim Garrison tried to have him extradited during the Shaw trial, Texas Governor John Connally refused to sign the extradition papers.

AOT - Page 56
C - Page 297
CF - Page 507
HT - Page 289
MK - Page 97
OTT - Page 305
RD - Page 290
SS - Page 35

Q. Who was Gordon Arnold?

A. He was a U.S. Army soldier home from basic training. He said he saw two men on the sixth floor of the Depository at 12:15 -- one holding a rifle . He was on the Grassy Knoll, felt a bullet fly past his left ear and immediately hit the ground.

AOT - Page 378
C - Page 24

CF - Page 78
COA - Page 41
HT - Page 462
RD - Page 112

Q. Who was Guy Banister?

A. A former FBI agent who later began a detective agency in New Orleans, he had ties to the CIA, anti-Castro Cubans, David Ferrie and Lee Oswald, and was suspected of being involved in the assassination. He died of an apparent heart attack in June 1964 before he could testify before the Warren Commission.

AOT - Page 44
C - Pages 290 & 489
CF - Page 559
COA - Page 61
DC - Page 332
FH - Page 50
HT - Page 154
HTII - Page 506
MK - Page 145
OTT - Pages 4-5
RD - Pages 289-90
SS - Page 33

Q. Who was Charles Batchelor?

A. He was the Dallas Assistant Chief of Police whose two assignments were security precautions for the motorcade and the handling of Oswald's transfer to the county jail. It has been suggested that he brought Jack Ruby into the police station to kill Oswald. He was later promoted to Chief of Police.

COA - Page 383
HT - Pages 188, 236, 293
HTII - Page 579
RC - Page 125

Q. Who was U.E. Baughman?

A. Chief of the Secret Service when JFK became President, he retired after 34 years of service. He was quoted as saying that there was no Mafia in the U.S. His successor was James J. Rowley who had been with the FBI in 1937, then transferred to the Secret Service White House detail in 1938. After the assassination, rumors circulated that a feud between the FBI and Secret Service had been a contributing factor in the President's death.

AOT - Page 101

Q. Who was Dave Beck?

A. He was President of the Teamsters Union. Convicted of larceny in state court and tax evasion in federal court, he went to prison in 1957. He was succeeded as teamsters president by Jimmy Hoffa. Gerald Ford granted Beck a full pardon in May 1975.

C - Page 244
CF - Page 167
DC - Page 232
FH - Page 219
MK - Page 87

Q. Who was David Belin?

A. Belin was one of the authors of the "single bullet theory". He was counsel for the Warren Commission, insisted that Oswald acted alone and that there was no conspiracy. He was quoted as saying that Congressman Henry Gonzales, the first Chairman of the House Select Committee on Assassinations, was wrong in asserting that a second gunman had fired at President Kennedy. Henry Gonzales was in the motorcade -- David Belin was not.

AOT - Page 495
BE - Page 98

Q. Who was Abraham Bolden?

A. He was the first black man hired as an agent by the Secret Service, appointed by President Kennedy. While stationed at the White House, he stated that the Secret Service operations were "terribly lax". He was promptly transferred to Chicago. While in Chicago, Bolden said he received an FBI teletype telling of a plot to shoot the President in Chicago. The FBI denies that such a teletype was sent. Bolden was indicted, tried, and imprisoned for allegedly accepting a bribe. Kennedy's Chicago trip was cancelled.

Q. Who was Jim Braden (his real name was Eugene Hale Brading)?

A. He was a Mafia operative and was arrested in Dealey Plaza moments after the assassination. It was later learned that he had visited the offices of H.L. Hunt at the same time Jack Ruby was there on 21 November 1963. He reportedly also had an office in New Orleans in the fall of 1963 just down the hall from David Ferrie. He had been given permission by his parole officer to travel to Texas on "oil business".

AOT - Page 308
C - Page 452
COA - Page 67
FH - Page 327
HT - Pages 121 & 305
MK - Page 208
OTT - Page 205
RC - Page 77
RD - Page 124

Q. Who was Dr. George Burkley and what did he later say about the assassination?

A. He was JFK's personal physician, rode in the motorcade, was at Parkland Hospital and accompanied the body to

Bethesda Naval Hospital where he was present at the autopsy. In 1982 he is said to have told author Henry Hurt that he felt the assassination had been a conspiracy.

BE - Page 45
CF - Page 371
HT - Page 87
HTII - Page 56

Q. Who was Charles Cabell?

A. He was a Deputy Director of the CIA in Clandestine Operations and was fired by JFK after the Bay of Pigs. His brother was Mayor of Dallas and some researchers believe he tried to undermine the President's Secret Service protection.

AOT - Page 121
CF - Page 562
DC - Page 300
HT - Pages 154 & 425
HTII - Page 562
MK - Page 369
OTT - Page 103
PD - Page 98
RD - Pages 282-283

Q. Who was Earle Cabell?

A. He was the Mayor of Dallas at the time of the assassination. Security for the motorcade was his responsibility.

AOT - Page 380
BE - Page 45
DC - Page 334
HT - Page 154
HTII - Page 87
OTT - Page 102

Q. Who was Rose Cheramie?

A. She was a prostitute, drug addict and alcoholic who was found injured on a road near Eunice, La. on the night of 20 November 1963. She said she had been with two "Latin men" travelling to Texas and had been left behind after a quarrel. She told doctors she heard the two men discussing the assassination plot. She was ignored by authorities.

C - Page 592
COA - Page 54
HT - Page 141
HTII - Page 77

MK - Page 194
RD - Page 411

Q. Who was Roger Craig?

A. He was a Dallas Deputy Sheriff who reported seeing a man run from the Texas School Book Depository and climb into a Rambler station wagon. He said that he saw the same man later in Captain Fritz' office and identified him as Oswald.

COA - Page 57
HT - Page 132
MK - Page 207
OTT - Page 94
RD - Page 102
SS - Page 110

Q. Who was Judge Hawk Daniels?

A. He was a federal investigator who later became a judge in Louisiana. He received information in 1962 regarding a death threat by Jimmy Hoffa which involved both John and Robert Kennedy.

C - Page 253
MK - Page 444

Q. Who was George DeMohrenschildt?

A. He was an exiled White Russian whose family had been members of the aristocracy, he was an oil geologist with ties to American intelligence who befriended Oswald and believed he was innocent. He was quoted in 1977 as saying that there had been a conspiracy in the assassination and that American intelligence was involved.

AOT - Page 156
C - Pages 193 & 492
CF - Pages 200, 278, & 565
COA - Page 58
DC - Page 332
FH - Page 34
HT - Pages 145, 189 & 299
HTII - Page 414
OTT - Page 51
PD - Page 32
RD - Page 219
SS - Page 76

Q. Who was Sylvia Duran?

A. She worked in the Cuban consul's office in Mexico City at the time Lee Oswald was supposed to have visited there requesting a visa to Cuba. When shown a filmed interview of Oswald after the assassination, she said that the man on the film did not look like the man she saw in Mexico City. The CIA had Mexican police officials arrest her twice. After the second arrest she wouldn't talk about her experiences.

AOT - Page 316
C - Pages 346-350
CF - Page 194
FH - Page 35
HT - Page 190
MK - Page 164
OTT - Page 64
PD - Page 46
RD - Page 232
SS - Page 97

Q. Who was Judith Campbell Exner?

A. She was an alleged mistress of President Kennedy at the same time she was sleeping with Chicago mobster Sam Giancana. She later said she had been a courier between the two for an eighteen month period.

AOT - Page 56
C - Pages 248-249 & 527
CF - Page 177
COA - Page 89
DC - Page 282
FH - Page 409
HTII - Page 578
K - Page 355
MK - Page 96
RD - Page 176

Q. Who was David Ferrie?

A. He was a former airline pilot with ties to anti-Castro Cubans, organized crime, and the CIA. He was friends with Guy Banister, Clay Shaw and had known Lee Oswald from the time he was a teenager in new Orleans. Ferrie was overheard to say that the President ought to be shot. He was to have been the star witness in Jim Garrison's case against Clay Shaw but mysteriously died before he could testify.

AOT - Page 64
C - Page 299
CF - Page 98
COA - Page 60
DC - Page 294

FH - Page 50
HT - Page 122
HTII - Page 416
MK - Page 144
OTT - Page 6
RD - Page 277
SS - Page 4

Q. Who was Captain Will Fritz?

A. He was the chief of the Dallas Police Homicide Bureau at the time of the assassination.

AOT - Page 393
BE - Page 351
C - Page 54
COA - Page 143
FH - Page 339
OTT - Page 22
SS - Page 123

Q. Who was Jim Garrison?

A. He was the former District Attorney of New Orleans, and
later a judge of the Court of Appeals. He was the only person
to bring anyone to trial for the assassination of JFK. That
person was Clay Shaw.

AOT - Page 44
BE - Page 386
FH - Page 49
HT - Page 135
HTII - Page 505
MK - Page 133
OTT
PD - Page 25
RC - Page 95
RD - Pages 261-289
SS - Page 35

Q. Who was Sam Giancana?

A. He was the Chicago Mafia boss involved with the CIA in
the Bay of Pigs invasion. He reportedly sent "Chuckie"
Nicoletti, "Milwaukee Phil" Alderisio and Richard Cain to
Dallas and claimed that Cain and Nicoletti were the gunmen
in the Texas School Book Depository. He said it was Cain,
not Oswald, who fired from the sixth floor.

Q. Who was Charles Harrelson?

A. He was convicted of having murdered Federal Judge John H. Wood, Jr. on 29 May 1979 in San Antonio, Texas and has admitted that he participated in the President's assassination. Sam Giancana told his brother Chuck that Carlos Marcello sent Harrelson and Jack Lawrence to Dallas as one of the shooting teams.

HTII - Page 77
MK - Page 208
RD - Page 349

Q. Who was Gerry Hemming?

A. He was a Marine, later recruited by Naval Intelligence, who believed Oswald was involved with the intelligence community. He has been referred to as a mercenary who participated in CIA-backed Cuban-Exile activities. He was the Marine sergeant over Oswald at Atsugi, Japan and identified by Marita Lorenz as one of a secret squad assigned to assassinate JFK.

C - Page 268
CF - Pages 204 & 398
COA - Page 225
FH - Page 197
HT - Page 392
PD - Pages 131 & 300
RD - Page 243

Q. Who was Hal Hendrix?

A. He was a Miami journalist who, when contacted by newspaper correspondent Seth Kantor on the afternoon of the assassination, was able to supply details of Oswald's past before they became common knowledge.

C - Pages 104-105
RC - Page 376

Q. Who was Jim Hicks?

A. He was possibly the man photographed in the Cuban and Soviet Embassies in Mexico, and he was identified incorrectly as Oswald. He was in Dealey Plaza on the day of the assassination and may have provided the radio communication for the snipers.

HT - Page 182

Q. Who was Jimmy Hoffa?

A. He was leader of the Teamsters Union and had contributed heavily to Nixon's 1960 Presidential campaign. He was indicted in Nashville for jury-tampering in May 1963 but was not sent to prison until March 1967 after exhausting all his appeals. He was pardoned by Richard Nixon on 23 December 1971.

Q. Who was Ed Hoffman?

A. He was the deaf-mute who saw men with guns behind the fence on the Grassy Knoll. He tried to alert authorities to what he had seen but was unable to make himself understood. He said that when he told the FBI what he had seen, one agent told him not to discuss it or "you might get killed". He also has said the FBI tried to pay him to keep silent.

Q. Who was J. Edgar Hoover?

A. He was the long-time Director of the FBI and one of the most feared men in Washington, D.C.

AOT
BE - Page 48
C - Page 259
COA - Page 38
DC - Page 132
DP - Page 143
FH - Page 18
HT - Page 74
HTII - Page 75
MK - Page 99
OTT - Page 50
PD - Page 20
RC - Page 27
RD - Page 6

Q. Who was H.L. Hunt?

A. He was one of the richest men in American and having made his fortune in oil, he was very concerned by President Kennedy's threat to disallow the oil depletion allowance. He reportedly watched the motorcade pass from his office in Dallas and was then flown to Mexico by the FBI within an hour after the assassination. He allegedly remained in Mexico for one month.

HT - Page 305

Q. Who was William Avery Hyde?

A. He was the father of Ruth Paine with whom Marina Oswald was living at the time of the assassination. He reportedly had intelligence connections and was allegedly acquainted with Oswald's friend George DeMohrenschildt.

HT - Page 300

Q. Who was Guy Johnson?

A. He was a Naval Intelligence reserve officer in New Orleans and Clay Shaw's first defense attorney when he was arrested by Garrison on 1 March 1967.

HT - Page 289
OTT - Pages 26& 145

Q. Who was Priscilla Johnson?

A. She was a journalist who befriended Marina Oswald after the assassination. She had ties to the CIA and State Department and had met Oswald in Moscow in 1959. The bus ticket stub which the Warren Commission used as evidence that Oswald had been in Mexico City, was found by Marina Oswald in a magazine during a visit from Johnson.

PD - Pages 48 & 67

Q. Who was Tom Karamessines?

A. He was an assistant to Richard Helms at the CIA and the alleged author of an internal CIA memorandum which said E. Howard Hunt was in Dallas on the day of the assassination.

FH - Page 88
HT - Page 345

Q. Who was Roy Kellerman?

A. He was the Secret Service Agent-in-Charge of the Presidential limousine, riding in the front seat with the driver. He told the Warren Commission, "if President Kennedy had from all reports four wounds, Governor Connally three, there have got to be more than three shots, gentlemen".

AOT - Page 351
BE - Page 286
C - Page 19
CF - Page 12
DP - Page 27
FH - Page 10
HT - Page 148
HTII - Page 71
OTT - Page 144
RD - Page 68

Q. Who was Jack Lawrence?

A. He had been employed at the Downtown Lincoln-Mercury for a month when the assassination occurred. He reportedly had come to Dallas from New Orleans, borrowed a car from the dealership the night before the President was killed, and returned "muddy and sweating profusely" within 30 minutes of the assassination. Sam Giancana alleged that Lawrence was sent along with Harrelson by Carlos Marcello to take part in the assassination.

DC - Page 334
HT - Page 133

Q. Who was James R. Leavelle?

A. He was the detective Oswald was handcuffed to during his attempted transfer to the Dallas county jail.

DP - Page 520
FH - Page 344
MK - Page 227
RC - Page 148
RTJ - Page 209

Q. Who was Marita Lorenz?

A. She reportedly had been Castro's lover, was recruited by the CIA to kill him and has stated that she travelled from Miami to Dallas with Frank Sturgis in November 1963 to assassinate JFK. She has said that Sturgis later confirmed his involvement and that Gerry Hemming was part of the team.

FH - Page 200
PD - Pages 288 & 295
RTJ - Page xv

Q. Who was Robert McClelland?

A. He was the general surgeon at Parkland Hospital and a reliable witness to the condition of the President's body.

AOT - Page 407
BE - Page 39
C - Page 479
DP - Page 524
HT - Page 451
HTII - Page 104
OTT - Page 91
PD - Page 355

Q. Who was William McKenzie?

A. He was a partner in the Wynne-McKenzie law firm and acted as Marina Oswald's attorney.

HT - Page 283

Q. Who was Robert Mahue?

A. He was an aide to Howard Hughes with close ties to the CIA. He worked closely with Charles Cabell in plots to eliminate Castro.

AOT - Page 64
C - Page 238
COA - Page 216
DC - Page 333
FH - Page 58
HT - Page 314
MK - Page 98
RC - Page 64

Q. Who was Dante Marachini?

A. He started work at the Reily Coffee Company in New Orleans on the same day as Oswald, lived next door to Clay Shaw, and was acquainted with David Ferrie. After Oswald's departure, he left to work for the National Aeronautics and Space Administration along with several other former Reily Coffee Company employees.

OTT - Page 115
SS - Page 43

Q. Who was Carlos Marcello?

A. He was the leader of the Mafia in New Orleans hiding under the guise of a tomato salesman. According to Sam

Giancana he sent Charles Harrelson and Jack Lawrence to Dallas to take part in the assassination.

AOT - Page 14
C - Page 256
CF - Pages 164-172
COA - Page 20
DC - Page 64
FH - Pages xxxix & 276
HT - Page 119
HTII - Page 416
K - Page 338
MK
OTT - Page 288
RC - Page 69
RD - Page 180

Q. Who was Victor Marchetti?

A. He was an assistant to CIA Director Richard Helms and he, in a published article, said that E. Howard Hunt had been in Dallas on the day of the assassination. It has been suggested that Hunt along with Charles Harrelson & Frank Sturgis of Watergate fame, were "the three tramps" arrested in the railroad yard following the assassination.

C - Page 143
CF - Page 188
HT - Page 144
OTT - Page 234
PD - Page 130
RD - Page 288

Q. Who was Jack Martin?

A. After being pistol-whipped by Guy Banister, his employer in New Orleans, he told police on November 22 that Banister and David Ferrie were involved in the assassination and that David Ferrie knew Oswald.

C - Page 303
CF - Page 492
FH - Page 50
HT - Page 186
HTTII - Page 506
MK - Page 205
OTT - Page 30

Q. Who was James Herbert Martin?

A. He was hired as Marina Oswald's "business manager" after the assassination.

AOT - Page 494
FH - Page 84
HT - Page 283

Q. Who was John Martino?

A. Martino worked for the Mafia running casinos in Havana before the revolution. He became involved with the CIA and William Pawley in anti-Castro activities. He reportedly said that Oswald didn't know who he was working for but was set up by anti-Castro people. He also said Oswald went to the Texas Theater to meet his "contact" (for purposes unknown).

C - Page 424
CF - Page 153
FH - Page 89
HT - Page 145

Q. Who was Ester Ann Mash?

A. In 1963 she was asked by Jack Ruby to serve drinks in his Carousel Club at a meeting which included five "gangster-types" from Chicago, along with Jack Ruby and Lee Oswald. She claimed they were discussing the assassination.

CF - Page 408

Q. Who was Teofil Meller?

A. A Dallas friend of Oswald who, in 1962, asked the FBI about Oswald, since he was a defector. The FBI said Oswald was alright.

AOT - Page 176
C - Page 104
FH - Page 379

Q. Who was Julia Ann Mercer?

A. She was a witness to the arrival of a young man with a rifle in a bag who left a pick-up truck near the underpass and climbed up to the Grassy Knoll. Later, when the pictures of Jack Ruby were shown on television she identified the pick-up driver as being Jack Ruby.

HT - Page 135
MK - Page 195

Q. Who was Joseph Milteer?

A. He was a wealthy, right-wing extremist who told a police informant in early November 1963 that the President was going to be shot "from a office building with a high-powered rifle". He reportedly was in Dallas on the day of the assassination. After the assassination he is said to have told the same informant that "everything ran true to form".

AOT - Page 352
C - Pages 404 & 624
CF - Pages 242 & 562
FH - Page 7HT - Pages 13 & 414
RD - Pages 127 & 410

Q. Who was John Mitchell?

A. Attorney-General under Nixon, he suppressed ballistic evidence regarding the assassination -- evidence which would have proven the presence of more than one gun.

Q. Who was Martha Mitchell?

A. Wife of Attorney-General Mitchell, she was disturbed by the secrecy of the Nixon Administration and tried to alert the news media to the Mafia ties to the Presidency.

Q. Who was Clint Murchison?

A. An oil magnate in Dallas, he was a close friend of Richard Nixon, J. Edgar Hoover, Jimmy Hoffa and Meyer Lansky -- Mafia financial brain. Author Penn Jones has claimed that Nixon and Hoover were guests in the Murchison home the evening before the assassination.

AOT - Page 56
COA - Page 244
DC - Page 332
HT - Page 282
MK - Page 347

Q. Who was Charles Nicoletti?

A. "Chuckie" Nicoletti reportedly was sent along with Richard Cain and "Milwaukee Phil" Alderisio by Sam Giancana to Dallas. Giancana claimed that both Cain and Nicoletti were the shooters from the Book Depository.

C - Page 494
COA - Page 452
DC - Page 334
HT - Page 369

Q. Who was Orville Nix?

A. He was an amateur photographer who filmed the assassination including the controversial frames showing the red brake lights remaining on until the fatal head shot. His film also shows flashes from the Grassy Knoll which could be rifle fire. Nix was never called to testify before the Warren Commission.

AOT - Page 398
BE - Page 10
CF - Page 35
HT - Page 224

Q. Who was Marguerite Oswald?

A. Lee's mother, who until she died professed his innocence and repeatedly stated that he had worked for the government. After the assassination neither of her two other sons or Lee's widow, Marina, had any further contact with her. She is buried beside Lee in Rose Hill Cemetery in Fort Worth.

AOT - Page 153
C - Page 129
COA - Page 65
DP - Page 90
FH - Page 38
HT - Page 164
MK - Page 139
OTT - Page 304
PD - Page 21
RC - Page 95

RD - Page 115
SS - Page 12

Q. Who was Ruth Paine?

A. She befriended Marina Oswald, and Marina and her daughters were living in her home in Irving, Texas at the time of the assassination. After the assassination Marina was "distanced" from Ruth.

AOT - Page 195
C - Page 369
DP - Page 95
HT - Page 300
OTT - Page 62
PD - Page 344
RC - Page 52
SS - Page 56

Q. Who was William Pawley?

A. He was a former American diplomat and founder of the Flying Tigers in World War II and was very involved in the anti-Castro movement. He was credited with persuading

Clare Booth Luce, influential wife of the chairman of Time, Inc. to finance anti-Castro operations.

C - Page 425
HT - Page 145

Q. Who was Carlos Prio?

A. A former President of Cuba with links to Jack Ruby, Frank Sturgis and top Mafia leaders. He was on the list of witnesses the House Select Committee on Assassinations had planned to interview but died first.

C - Page 493
CF - Page 565
FH - Page 197
HT - Page 145

Q. Who was Delphine Roberts?

A. Guy Banister's secretary, she stated that she saw Lee Oswald in Banister's New Orleans office several times in 1963. She felt he was "required to act undercover".

AOT - Page 265
C - Page 295
FH - Page 189
HT - Page 289
HT II - Page 513
MK - Page 205
OTT - Page 43
RD - Page 291
SS - Page 34

Q. Who was Johnny Roselli?

A. A Las Vegas Mafia figure who was involved in the CIA-backed Bay of Pigs invasion along with Sam Giancana and Santos Trafficante.

AOT - Page 116
C - Page 495
COA - Page 58
DC - Page 72
FH - Page 58
HT - Page 154
HTII - Page 414
MK - Page 97
OTT - Page 76
RC - Page 76
RD - Page 176

Q. Who was Clay Shaw?

A. He was a prominent New Orleans businessman with connections to the CIA and David Ferrie, and the only person brought to trial for involvement in the assassination. Unfortunately, the case against him was not strong enough and he was acquitted.

C - Page 306
CF - Page 68
COA - Page 70
FH - Page 52
HT - Pages 144-145
HTII - Page 507
MK - Page 146
OTT - Beginning page 75
PD - Page 25
RD - Pages 265-278
SS - Page 25

Q. Who was William Somersett?

A. He was an informant for the Miami Police and for the FBI who was told about the assassination plans by Joseph Milteer. That information was apparently ignored. According to authors Groden and Livingstone Somersett's safety was compromised by those he was providing information to. They reportedly told Milteer that Somersett was informing on him. On 3 April 1968 Somersett called Miami Police Detective Lt. C.H. Sapp and told him he had heard of a plot to kill Dr. Martin Luther King in Memphis the next day. Again his information was apparently ignored and Dr. King died.

AOT - Page 352
HT - Beginning Page 474

Q. Who was Lou Staples?

A. He was a radio talk-show host in Dallas who told friends about his plans to solve the assassination.

CF - Page 565

Q. Who was William Sullivan?

A. J. Edgar Hoover's number three man who headed the FBI's Counter-Espionage and Domestic Intelligence Division. He and CIA Counter-Intelligence Chief James Angleton reportedly rehearsed the questions and answers they planned to give Warren Commission investigators. The circumstances surrounding his death are also mysterious.

Q. Who was Santos Trafficante?

A. He was the head of the Mafia in Florida and reportedly was involved with plans for the Bay of Pigs invasion along with Sam Giancana and Johnny Roselli. He reportedly was quoted prior to the assassination as saying President Kennedy "was going to be hit." He may also have been responsible for Johnny Roselli's death.

RC - Page 40
RD - Page 178

Q. Who was Antonio Veciana?

A. A Cuban exile and founder of Alpha 66, an active anti-Castro group. He had CIA connections and identified the name "Maurice Bishop" as being the code name for his intelligence contact. He was shot in the head after testifying before the House Committee but survived.

C - Page 324
CF - Page 149
HT - Page 286
MK - Page 439
RD - Page 327

Q. Who was Roscoe White?

A. According to his son Ricky, Roscoe fired the fatal shot from the Grassy Knoll and later shot Officer Tippit. Sam

Giancana alleged that White and Tippit were sent as gunmen by the CIA, that Tippit was supposed to have killed Oswald and, when Oswald got away, White had to kill Tippit. Ricky also has stated that Roscoe killed 28 witnesses.

Austin American-Statesman - August 5 & 7, 1990
DC - Page 335
HTII - Page 463

The Autopsy

Q. How was the investigation into President Kennedy's death first mishandled?

A. Secret Service agents removed the President's body from Parkland Hospital before an autopsy could be performed, (as required under Texas law), which resulted in an inadequate autopsy at Bethesda Naval Hospital.

BE - Page 389
HT - Page 266
OTT - Page 243

Q. Who ordered the removal of President Kennedy's body from Parkland before the autopsy could be performed?

A. President Johnson.

CF - Page 586

Q. What was different about the way in which President Kennedy's body arrived at Bethesda Naval Hospital compared to the way it left Dallas?

A. It allegedly left Dallas wrapped in a sheet in a bronze ceremonial casket. It reportedly arrived at Bethesda in a body bag in a metal shipping casket.

BE - Page 595
HT - Page 454

Q. Were the doctors who performed the autopsy qualified?

A. Not according to several experts including Dr. Milton Halpern, the former Medical Examiner for New York City. Neither Navy doctor had ever performed an autopsy and no specialized help was provided.

BE - Page 529
C - Page 8
HT - Page 265

Q. Was the President's autopsy sabotaged?

A. Authors Groden and Livingstone say it was deliberately sabotaged. The autopsy was prevented from following proper procedure by military officers and others in attendance.

HT - Page 264

Q. Were regulations followed in making the autopsy report?

A. No. The x-rays and autopsy photographs were not attached as required.

BE - Page 80
HT - Page 267

Q. Was the autopsy report altered?

A. Forensic scientist Charles Wilbur believes that the report was altered enroute through military channels. The President's personal physician, Admiral George Burkley, admitted that he altered the report.

BE - Page 169
HT - Page 110

Q. What did Dr. James Humes, who performed the Kennedy autopsy with Dr. Thornton Boswell, do with his original autopsy notes?

A. For unexplained reasons he burned them in his fireplace.

BE - Page 5
CF - Page 374
HT - Page 87

Q. Was film of the autopsy deliberately exposed to light?

A. Yes. Reportedly film was taken from a Navy corpsman by Secret Service agents and exposed to light.

HT - Page 86

Q. What did witnesses at Bethesda say the Navy corpsman on duty photographed?

A. The autopsy activities and the individuals in attendance.

HT - Page 86

Q. What did Dr. Humes say happened to the x-rays and photographs?

A. He testified that they were not developed and had been turned over to either the Secret Service or FBI on the night of the autopsy.

HT - Page 85

Q. Was autopsy evidence changed?

A. Yes. According to researchers the Warren Commission members were shown drawings of the wounds which witnesses claim did not depict the wounds accurately.

BE
HT - Page 268

Q. Was Earl Warren allowed to see all the autopsy evidence?

A. No, reportedly he was only allowed to see the photograph of the back of the head and the x-rays.

HT - Page 83

114

Q. Were there any wounds at the front of the President's head?

A. Dr. Boswell reportedly drew a picture of a wound in the left temple area but it was omitted from the autopsy report.

BE
HT - Page 264 & 267

Q. Were standard procedures followed during the autopsy?

A. No. The doctors were given "unlawful orders" thus omitting certain procedures which should have been performed. These "orders" were against military regulations.

BE - Page 611
HT - Page 267

Q. Were members of the autopsy team threatened with court-martial if they revealed any information?

A. Yes.

HT - Page 57 & 267

Q. Have any autopsy witnesses ever spoken publicly?

A. Yes but not until twenty-five years after the assassination.

HT - Pages 447 & 458

Q. Were the autopsy photographs forged?

A. Yes. The gaping wound or "defect" in the back of the head is not shown in any autopsy photographs.

HT - Page 268

Q. What is wrong with the autopsy photographs?

A. They show only a small entry wound at the back of the skull and not the large "defect" described by eyewitnesses.

HT - Pages 38 & 455

Q. Were the Kennedy autopsy x-rays tampered with?

116

A. Yes, several researchers have said they are not x-rays of President Kennedy. The head x-rays are totally incompatible with autopsy photographs which show an undamaged face.

HT - Page 82

Q. Were any pieces of lead removed from the President's body during the autopsy?

A. Yes, according to autopsy witness Dennis David, four large pieces of lead were removed from the head. He said they had jagged edges like shrapnel.

HT - Page 267

The Patsy

Q. What sort of person was Oswald?

A. The American people were led to believe that Lee Oswald was a lonely, left-wing nut and a school drop-out. Actually, he was very intelligent. Many researchers now believe he was being used and manipulated by forces within our intelligence community.

C - Beginning Page 264
CF - Page 285
DC - Page 333

Q. Did Oswald serve in the Armed Forces?

A. Yes. He joined the Marine Corps and graduated 7th in his class.

SS - Page 7
TC - Page 30

Q. How did Oswald perform in the Marine Corps?

A. He enlisted at age 17, trained in radar and air traffic control and when further assignments required a security check, he passed it. He was stationed at Atsugi, Japan, a top secret installation which was the home of the U-2 spy plane.

C - starting Page 113
SS - Page 7

Q. Where did Oswald learn to speak Russian?

A. It is believed that he attended the Defense Language Institute in Monterey, California while he was in the Marine Corps. He became so proficient that when his Russian wife Marina first met him she thought he was Russian.

CF - Page 105
DC - Page 331
OTT - Page 22

Q. Was Lee Oswald fluent in languages other than English and Russian?

A. According to Nelson Delgado who served in the Marine Corps with Oswald he also spoke Spanish fluently.

OTT - Page 46

Q. Did Oswald ever talk to fellow Marines about his plans to go to Russia?

A. Yes, he told a Marine named Bucknell that American intelligence was sending him and that he would return a hero.

CF - Page 110

Q. Did any other Americans defect at about the same time as Oswald?

A. Yes. A former Navy man named Robert Webster defected less than two weeks before Oswald. He returned from Russia two weeks before Oswald.

C - Page 148
CF - Page 116

Q. Was Oswald in Russia at the time Gary Powers'* U-2 spy plane was shot down?

A. Yes, and Powers suspected Oswald might have given the Russians the information they would need. Colonel Fletcher Prouty says Powers' U-2 was flying below its operational altitude at the time it was brought down.

C - Pages 174 & 175

Q. Was anyone using Oswald's name while he was in Russia?

A. Reportedly a group of men tried to buy several trucks at Bolton Ford, Inc. in New Orleans on 20 January 1961 and asked that the purchase order documents have the name Oswald on them.

AOT - Page 63
OTT - Page 57

Q. Was Lee Harvey Oswald a spy?

A. All evidence indicates that he was an intelligence agent for the United States.

C - Beginning Page 60
CF - Pages 189-191
DC - Page 331
OTT - Pages 55 & 70
RD - Page 242

Q. Did Oswald have ties to the CIA?

A. Yes. A former finance officer in 1978 said Oswald had been recruited from the military for the express purpose of becoming a double-agent assigned to the USSR.

C - Page 129
DC - Page 331
OTT - Page 49
RD - Page 246

Q. Was Oswald an FBI informant?

A. The Warren Commission was informed on 22 January 1964 that authorities in Texas had information confirming that fact. Allen Sweatt, chief of the Dallas sheriff's office's criminal division told Secret Service agents that Oswald was being paid $200 per month by the FBI.

AOT - Page 512
CF - Page 472
OTT - Page 225
PD - Page 55
FBI Memo

Q. Did Oswald have a secret source of income while living in Russia?

A. Yes. Although Oswald called it his "Red Cross" money he said that it had come from the Soviet Secret Police after he had denounced the United States.

CF - Page 121

Q. Do we know what Oswald's life was like in Minsk?

A. He had a luxurious flat, far beyond the means of the average metalworker, and reportedly was making more money than the director of the factory where he was employed.

CF - Page 122
FH - Page 33

Q. Was it difficult for Oswald to return to the United States from Russia?

A. No, his passport was returned and he was even loaned repatriation money by the State Department.

C - Page 179
OTT - Page 51

Q. Were the Oswalds "debriefed" on their way back from Russia?

A. They reportedly stopped over in Amsterdam in private accommodations where their hosts spoke English. The chief council of the Warren Commission had no explanation for this detour.

CF - Page 127

Q. What was unusual about the Oswalds return from Russia?

A. Apparently they had seven suitcases when they arrived in New York. When they left New York they had five, and when they arrived in Fort Worth there were only two.

CF - Page 128
SS - Page 19

Q. What job did Lee Oswald obtain in Dallas in October 1962?

A. He was hired at Jagger-Stovall-Chiles, a firm which was under contract with the Pentagon to produce charts and maps for the military. Oswald was employed within one week of arriving in Dallas and apparently had access to classified materials.

DC - Page 332
OTT - Page 52
RD - Page 219

Q. Did the Oswalds have friends in the Russian community of Dallas?

A. According to Jim Garrison they were made welcome by the White Russian community which was unusual since the White Russians were anti-communist.

FH - Page 34

OTT - Page 53

Q. Since Oswald was a former defector, did any of his acquaintances in Dallas check him out with authorities before befriending him?

A. Yes. Teofil Meller* said he was told by the FBI in 1962 that "Oswald was all right". George DeMohrenschildt* claimed that he checked with an agent of the CIA's Domestic Contact Service and was told "Yes, he is okay. He is just a harmless lunatic."

C - Page 104

Q. Was Oswald a proficient marksman?

A. No. According to Marines with whom he served he got a lot of "Maggie's drawers" -- the red flag which is waved when a target is missed completely.

C - Page 74
CF - Page 102
HT - Page 176
OTT - Page 45
RD - Page 99

TC - Page 45

Q. Did Lee Oswald ever meet with Guy Banister* and David
Ferrie*?

A. Jim Garrison was told by Jack Martin* that the three had
met more than once in Banister's office at 544 Camp Street.

DC - Page 332
OTT - Page 32

Q. What was the "Fair Play for Cuba Committee"?

A. It was a pro-Castro group which Oswald joined. He was
its only member in New Orleans.

C - Page 268
HT - Page 309

Q. Were any U.S. Intelligence organizations involved with
the Fair Play for Cuba Committee?

A. According to author Anthony Summers there is documentation which proves that the Fair Play for Cuba Committee had been "penetrated" by the CIA and that Army Intelligence had an "operational interest" in the organization.

C - Page 275

Q. Was it common practice for U.S. undercover agents to infiltrate subversive groups?

A. Yes. We now know that subversive groups were routinely infiltrated in the interest of "national security".

C - Page 276

Q. Did Oswald have any contact with the FBI in the summer of 1963?

A. Yes. On 10 August 1963, while in police custody after being arrested in a street fight in New Orleans, he requested a meeting with the FBI. Special Agent John Quigley spent an hour and a half with him.

C - Page 280

Q. Was Oswald ever under FBI surveillance?

A. Yes, reportedly starting in May 1963 while he was in New Orleans.

AOT - Page 270

Q. Was Oswald questioned by the FBI prior to the assassination?

A. Yes. According to author Mark Lane he was questioned one week before the assassination.

PD - Page 350

Q. Was Lee Oswald ever in Mexico City?

A. We don't know. A man identifying himself as Oswald appeared at the Cuban consul's office on 27 September 1963 and created a scene when he wasn't given an immediate visa to Cuba. When later shown a filmed interview of Oswald, Sylvia Duran*, the consul's assistant, said he was not the same man she had seen.

Douglass Hubbard, 1962

Top: President Kennedy visited Yosemite National Park in August 1962. That visit was photographed by the author's father shown here. Bottom: Second and third from the left, back row, the author and her mother.

Top: President Kennedy with Richard Nixon.
Bottom: President Kennedy with Allen Dulles.

Top: President Kennedy with J. Edgar Hoover.
Bottom: Robert F. Kennedy with Jimmy Hoffa.

Top left: "Milwaukee Phil" Alderisio. Top right: James Angleton. Bottom left: Sergio Archaca-Smith. Bottom right: Guy Banister.

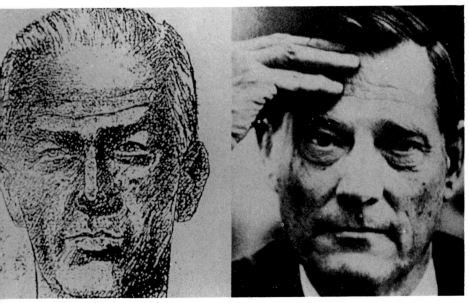

Top left: Charles Batchelor. Top right: Tippit murder witness Domingo Benavides. Bottom left: Alleged Veciana CIA contact Maurice Bishop. Bottom right: CIA employee David Atlee Phillips.

Top left: Hale Boggs. Top right: Eyewitness Lee Bowers.
Bottom left: Jim Braden. Bottom right: Eyewitness Howard
Brennan.

Top left: Anti-Castro Cuban Carlos Bringuier got into a scuffle with Oswald in New Orleans over Fair Play for Cuba. Top right: General Charles Cabell. Bottom left: Richard Cain. Bottom right: Rose Cheramie.

President and Mrs. Kennedy with Governor John Connally at Love Field.

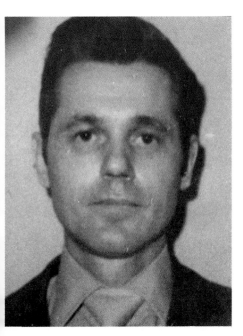

Top center: Dallas Police Chief Jesse Curry. Bottom left: Roger Craig. Bottom right: Judge Hawk Daniels.

137

Top left: Thomas E. Davis. Top right: George De-Mohrenschildt. Bottom left: George and Jeanne De-Mohrenschildt. Bottom right: Allen Dulles.

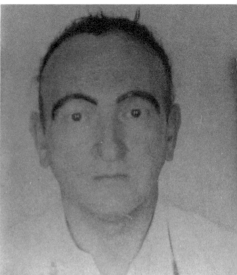
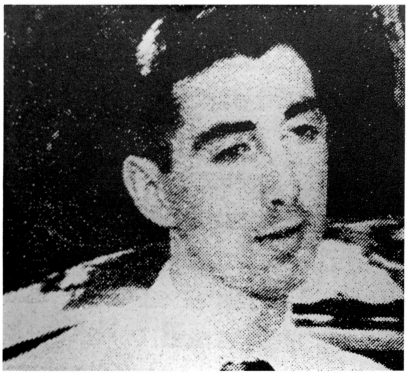

Top left: Judith Campbell Exner. Top right: David Ferrie.
Bottom center: Wesley Frazier.

139

Top left: Dallas Police Captain Will Fritz. Top right: Charles Harrelson. Bottom center: Jim Garrison.

140

Top left: Richard Helms. Top right: Gerry Hemming.
Bottom center: Eyewitness Jean Hill.

Top left: Jim Hicks. Top right: J. Edgar Hoover.
Bottom center: Eyewitness S.M. Holland.

Top left: James Hosty. Top right: E. Howard Hunt. Bottom left: Hank Killam and his wife Wanda Joyce. Bottom right: Jack Lawrence.

Top left: G. Gordon Liddy. Top right: Robert Mahue.
Bottom left: Carlos Marcello. Bottom right: M.N. Mc-
Donald, Oswald's arresting officer at the Texas Theater.

144

Marita Lorenz and Fidel Castro.

Top left: Victor Marchetti. Top right: Ruby's friend R.D.
Mathews. Bottom left: Mary Pinchot Meyer. Bottom right:
Joseph Milteer.

Top left: Chuckie Nicoletti. Top right: Eyewitness Orville
Nix. Bottom left: Eyewitness Beverly Oliver. Bottom right:
Marina Oswald.

Top: Ruth Paine.
Bottom: Paine house in Irving.

148

Top left: Jack Revill. Top right: Guy Banister's secretary Delphine Roberts. Bottom left: Johnny Roselli. Bottom right: Jack Ruby.

Top left: Richard Russell. Top right: Richard Schweiker.
Bottom center: Clay Shaw.

150

Top left: Arlen Specter. Top right: Frank Sturgis. Bottom left: William Sullivan. Bottom right: J.D. Tippit.

Top left: Santos Trafficante. Top right: Antonio Veciana.
Bottom left: Henry Wade. Bottom right: General Edwin
Walker.

Buddy Walters retrieving .45 caliber slug.

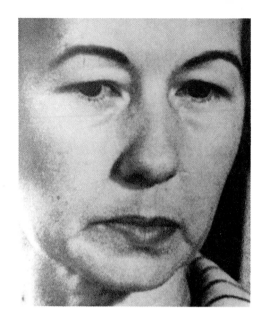

WILLIAM WHALEY

Top left: Eyewitness Carolyn Walther. Top right: William Whaley. Bottom center: Seymour Weitzman.

154

Roscoe White.

Top: General Walker's home.
Bottom: Eisenhower Gettysburg farm.

Top: Clay Shaw's home in New Orleans (center of photo).
Bottom: Guy Banister's office building on Camp Street.

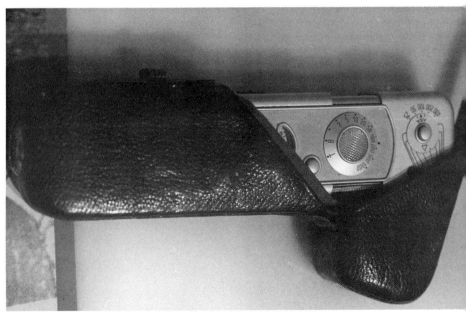

Top: Lee Harvey Oswald in the Marine Corps (bottom center of photo). Bottom: Minox "spy" camera.

Top: Oswald's apartment building in Minsk.
Bottom: U-2 spy plane.

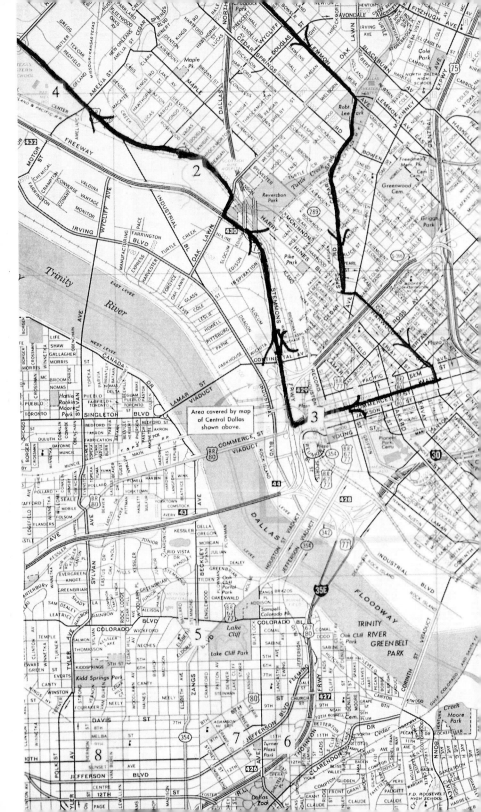

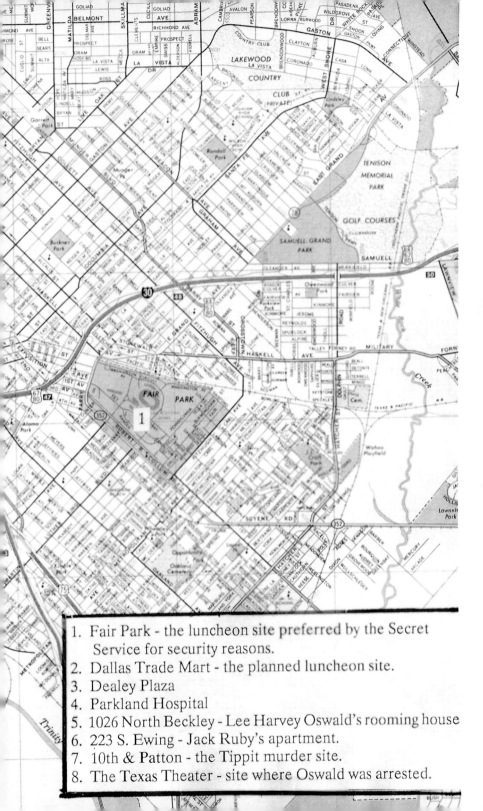

1. Fair Park - the luncheon site preferred by the Secret Service for security reasons.
2. Dallas Trade Mart - the planned luncheon site.
3. Dealey Plaza
4. Parkland Hospital
5. 1026 North Beckley - Lee Harvey Oswald's rooming house
6. 223 S. Ewing - Jack Ruby's apartment.
7. 10th & Patton - the Tippit murder site.
8. The Texas Theater - site where Oswald was arrested.

Lee Harvey Oswald handing out Fair Play for Cuba leaflets in New Orleans.

Top left: Lee Harvey Oswald. Top right: Marina and Lee
Oswald. Bottom center: The Dallas Trade Mart, planned site
for the luncheon.

Top: President and Mrs. Kennedy at Love Field.
Bottom: Motorcade in Dallas.

164

Top: Left to right - Secret Service agents Clint Hill, Roy Kellerman and William Greer. Bottom: The motorcade nears the Grassy Knoll, President Kennedy has been hit in the throat.

Top: President Kennedy has been shot. Notice what appears to be a head behind the fence on the Grassy Knoll (outlined in white). Bottom: Agent Clint Hill climbing on to the limousine.

Top left: Criminal Courts Building and Old Courthouse -- flags at half-mast. Top right: Left to right - Texas School Book Depository, Dal-Tex Building and County Records Building. Bottom: Aerial view of Dealey Plaza locating witnesses positions.

Emmett Hudson

Newmans

Zapruder's posi

Brehm and son

Jean Hill (left)

Mary Moorman (right)

Kennedy's location at fatal shot

Top: Grassy Knoll locating witnesses. Bottom: Motorcade on Stemmons Freeway.

Top left: Parkland Hospital emergency entrance. Top right: Bethesda Naval Hospital. Bottom: Parkland doctors, left Kemp Clark, far right Malcolm Perry.

Top: Grassy Knoll. Note sewer opening in curb below lamp post. Bottom: View from sewer on Elm Street where possible pistol shots could have originated.

Author Penn Jones climbing into sewer on Elm Street. Note Texas School Book Depository in background.

Top: Acoustics testing on the Grassy Knoll.
Bottom left: Texas School Book Depository from behind
picket fence on Grassy Knoll. Bottom right: TSBD from
Main and Houston Streets.

172

Top left: County Criminal Courts Building which houses the County jail and the Sheriff's office. Top right: Dallas County Records Building. Bottom: Police officers outside the Texas School Book Depository.

Top: Union Terminal North Tower where Lee Bowers was working. Bottom: Tramps arrested in the railroad yard.

Top left: Oswald's rooming house at 1026 N. Beckley in Oak Cliff. Top right: Texas Theater. Bottom: Tippit murder scene.

Top: Clint Murchison and wife.
Bottom: H.L. Hunt.

176

Top: Roscoe White's wife Geneva with Jack Ruby (she was employed by Ruby). Bottom: Jack Ruby at the Carousel Club.

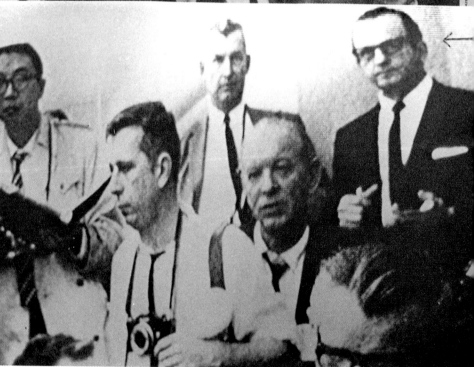

Top: Roger Craig in Captain Fritz's office. Bottom: Jack Ruby at the Friday night press conference.

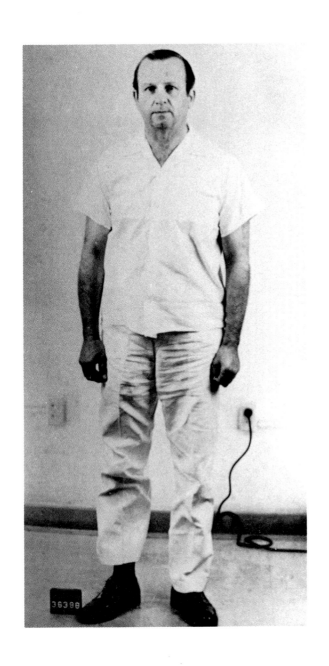

Jack Ruby after his arrest.

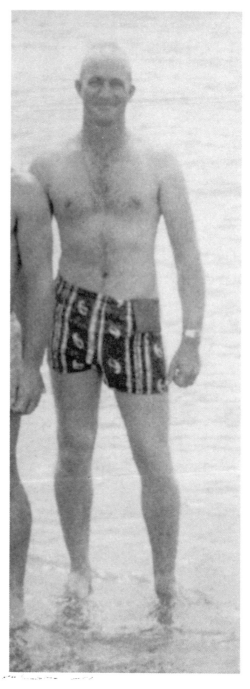

Roscoe White. Researcher Jack White reportedly has determined that the body in the "backyard photograph" of Lee Oswald at right, is actually that of Roscoe White.

180

Lee Harvey Oswald's face from mid-chin up -- Roscoe White's body from lower chin down.

181

CASE OF J.D. TIPPIT (DECEASED), JOHN F. KENNEDY (DECEASED) AND 7992
LEE OSWALD (SUSPECT)

DALLAS CITY-COUNTY CRIMINAL INVESTIGATION LABORATORY
DCCCIL __3531__

MISCELLANEOUS EXAMINATION REPORT CHEMICAL, TOXICOLOGICAL, ETC.

Specimen: (Use attached sheet for complete description, if necessary.)	
Ex #1: One manila envelope containing a paraffin cast of the right side of the face of Lee Oswald.	Date Received 11/23/63
	Delivered by (B. G. Brown
	(G. H. Doughty
Ex #2: One manila envelope containing a paraffin cast of the left hand of Lee Oswald.	Received by (L. Anderson
	(
Ex #3: One manila envelope containing a paraffin cast of the right hand of Lee Oswald.	

Envelope identification:
Ex #1: DALL BGB 11-23-63 GMD   11-22-63 WEB - JBHicks Right Side of face
Ex #2: OSS 7992 11-22-63 WEB JBHicks left Hand EX#2 BGB 11-23-63 GMD
Ex #3: 11-22-63 WEB J.B.Hicks Right Hand OSS 7992 EX#3 BGB 11-23-63 GMD

Examination Requested: Determine if nitrates are present on Exhibits #1, 2 and 3.

Requested by: Dallas Police Department.

Result of Examination:

No nitrates were found on Exhibit #1.

Nitrate patterns consistent with the subject having discharged a firearm were present on Exhibits #2 and 3. The pattern on Exhibit #3 is typical of the patterns produced in firing a revolver.

Analyst: Louie L. Anderson

Methods:
(1) Diphenylbenzidine test.

Dallas City-County Criminal
Investigation Laboratory

Date: 11/23/63

Report to: Lt. J. C. Day

Specimen to: Discarded.

Exhibits: Sketches of nitrate
patterns of casts.

The nitrate testing on Lee Harvey Oswald determined that he had not fired a rifle.

182

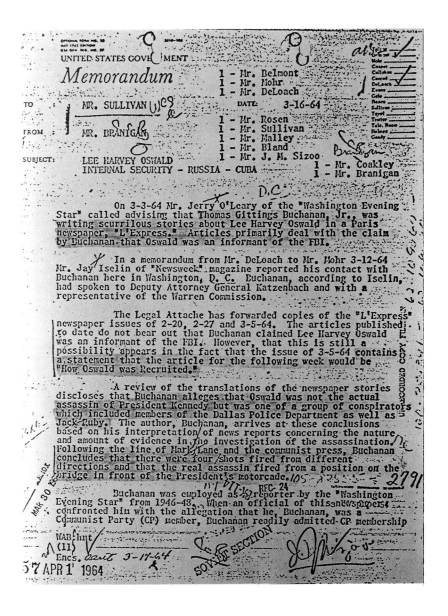

UNITED STATES GOVERNMENT

Memorandum

	1 - Mr. Belmont
	1 - Mr. Mohr
	1 - Mr. DeLoach

TO : MR. SULLIVAN   DATE: 3-16-64

	1 - Mr. Rosen
FROM : MR. BRANIGAN	1 - Mr. Sullivan
	1 - Mr. Malley
	1 - Mr. Bland
SUBJECT: LEE HARVEY OSWALD	1 - Mr. J. M. Sizoo
INTERNAL SECURITY - RUSSIA - CUBA	1 - Mr. Coakley
	1 - Mr. Branigan

D.C.

On 3-3-64 Mr. Jerry O'Leary of the "Washington Evening
Star" called advising that Thomas Gittings Buchanan, Jr., was
writing scurrilous stories about Lee Harvey Oswald in a Paris
newspaper, "L'Express." Articles primarily deal with the claim
by Buchanan that Oswald was an informant of the FBI.

In a memorandum from Mr. DeLoach to Mr. Mohr 3-12-64
Mr. Jay Iselin of "Newsweek" magazine reported his contact with
Buchanan here in Washington, D. C. Buchanan, according to Iselin,
had spoken to Deputy Attorney General Katzenbach and with a
representative of the Warren Commission.

The Legal Attache has forwarded copies of the "L'Express"
newspaper issues of 2-20, 2-27 and 3-5-64. The articles published
to date do not bear out that Buchanan claimed Lee Harvey Oswald
was an informant of the FBI. However, that this is still a
possibility appears in the fact that the issue of 3-5-64 contains
a statement that the article for the following week would be
"How Oswald was Recruited."

A review of the translations of the newspaper stories
discloses that Buchanan alleges that Oswald was not the actual
assassin of President Kennedy but was one of a group of conspirators
which included members of the Dallas Police Department as well as
Jack Ruby. The author, Buchanan, arrives at these conclusions
based on his interpretation of news reports concerning the nature
and amount of evidence in the investigation of the assassination.
Following the line of Mark Lane and the communist press, Buchanan
concludes that there were four shots fired from different
directions and that the real assassin fired from a position on the
bridge in front of the President's motorcade.

Buchanan was employed as a reporter by the "Washington
Evening Star" from 1946-48. When an official of this newspaper
confronted him with the allegation that he, Buchanan, was a
Communist Party (CP) member, Buchanan readily admitted CP membership

WAB:hmt
(11)
Encs.

57 APR 1 1964

FBI Soviet Section memorandum dated 16 March 1964
regarding the possibility that Oswald had been an FBI informant.

Top: Warren Commission, from left: Gerald Ford, Hale Boggs, Richard Russell, Chief Justice Earl Warren, John Sherman Cooper, John J. McCloy, Allen Dulles and chief counsel J. Leo Rankin. Bottom: From left - John Sherman Cooper, Richard Russell and Hale Boggs.

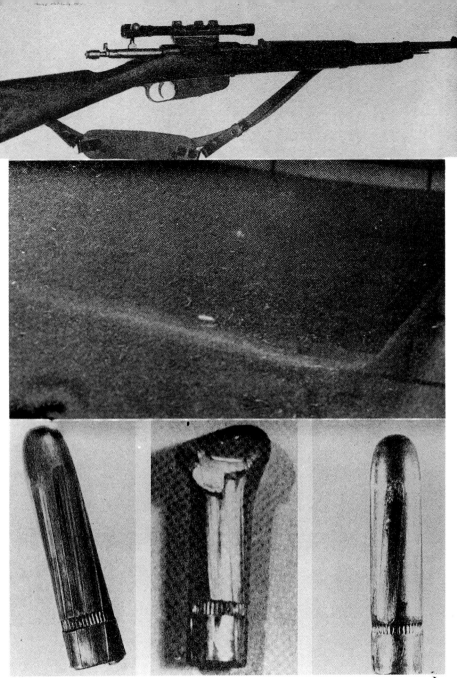

Top: The alleged murder weapon. Center: "Pristine" bullet on the stretcher at Parkland Hospital. Bottom: Left - Magic Bullet, center, test bullet after having been fired through a cadaver, right, bullet fired into water by author Henry Hurt.

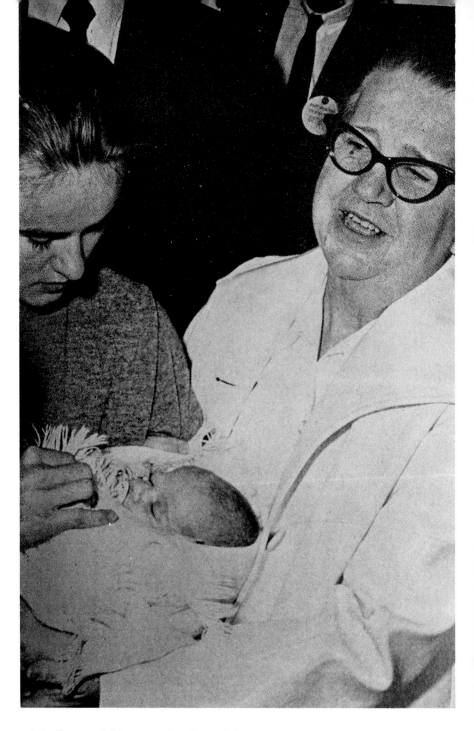

Marina and Marguerite Oswald.

Lee Harvey Oswald in custody.

Jack Ruby steps forward to shoot Oswald.

Lee Oswald in his coffin.

Marina, Robert and Marguerite Oswald attend Lee's funeral.

Robert Kennedy and Jacqueline Kennedy watch the President's coffin being loaded into a waiting hearse at Andrew's Air Force Base.

C - Page 345
RD - Page 231

Q. Did the FBI have information regarding Oswald's alleged visit to Mexico City?

A. Yes. According to author Summers, an FBI document prepared by Hoover within twenty-four hours of the assassination stated the CIA reported that on 1 October 1963 a sensitive source advised that someone identifying himself as Oswald had contacted the Soviet Embassy in Mexico City. Special agents of the bureau concluded that this individual was not Oswald.

C - Page 360
FH - Page 38

Q. Was someone impersonating Oswald before the assassination?

A. An Oswald look-alike was spotted in several different places including a gun and furniture store in Dallas, a car dealership in Dallas and the VA office in Austin.

C - Page 350, 375, 398
HT - Page 190, 352

Q. Did U.S. Army Intelligence have a file on Oswald?

A. Reportedly they did have but said it was "destroyed routinely in accordance with normal files management".

C - Page 276

Q. Did Oswald have a personal motive for killing JFK?

A. None that was ever proven. In fact, many people had the clear impression that he admired the President.

C - Page 99

Q. Where was Oswald seen in the Texas School Book Depository prior to the assassination?

A. Carolyn Arnold, who was secretary to the Vice-President of the Texas School Book Depository, said she saw him at about 12:15 or maybe slightly later in the second floor lunchroom. He was also seen in the lunchroom by Dallas Police Officer Baker just moments after the assassination.

C - Page 77
HT - Page 23 & 175
OTT - Page 100

Q. When did Lee Harvey Oswald first become a suspect?

A. A description matching Oswald's was broadcast by the Dallas police just before 12:45 p.m., fifteen minutes after the shots were fired in Dealey Plaza. This was one half hour before Dallas Police Officer J.D. Tippit was slain. Tippit's murder was what Oswald was originally arrested for.

RTJ - Page 81

Q. Did Oswald shoot Officer Tippit?

A. No. According to various sources he didn't have enough time to have left his rooming house, shot Tippit, and then walked to the Texas Theater where he was arrested. More importantly, Oswald did not fit the description given by witnesses. If Sam Giancana* was correct, Tippit was killed by Roscoe White*.

C - Beginning Page 85
DC - Page 335
HT - Pages 176, 238 & 239
OTT - Page 193
RD - Beginning 142

Q. Was a Dallas police car seen in front of Oswald's rooming house after the assassination?

A. According to Oswald's landlady, Earlene Roberts, a police car pulled slowly up, the horn honked and then the car slowly drove away.

TC - Page 204

Q. Was nitrate testing done to determine if Oswald had fired a rifle recently?

A. Yes. Tests on his cheeks were negative. There were traces of nitrate on his hands which could have come from touching items in the Texas School Book Depository.

C - Page 75
HT - Page 175
OTT - Page 100

Q. Did Oswald claim that photographs showing him holding a rifle and gun were faked?

A. Yes, he said that it was his face but not his body and that he had never seen the picture before.

C - Beginning Page 64
HT - Pages 199-201
SS - Page 117

Q. Was Oswald questioned without having a lawyer present?

A. According to Mark Lane he was questioned for 48 hours without legal representation.

PD - Page 352

Q. Did the FBI record the interrogation of Oswald?

A. No. According to author Mark Lane they refused to tape it and no transcript exists.

PD - Page 17

Q. Was Oswald telling the truth when he said "I didn't shoot anybody"?

A. Yes, according to tapes which have been examined with Psychological Stress Evaluators by George O'Toole, formerly with the CIA, Oswald was telling the truth.

HT - Page 349

Q. Did Captain Fritz* ever refuse to transfer Oswald to the county jail?

A. According to author Mark Lane he refused more than once. He was asked by the Dallas District Attorney to transfer Oswald on 22 November and on 23 November Chief Curry asked that the prisoner be transferred at 4 p.m. that day. Both requests were denied.

FH - Page 342
RTJ - Page 215

Q. Were the FBI and Dallas County Sheriff's office warned that Oswald would be killed?

A. Yes. On the morning of 24 November 1964. The deputy who received the anonymous telephone call later recognized the voice as being that of Jack Ruby.

RC - Page 276
RTJ - Page 209

Q. Were the security arrangements adequate for Oswald's transfer to the county jail?

A. No. Reportedly Chief Curry refused Captain Fritz' request to transfer Oswald in an armored car and he didn't even have a "human shield" to protect Oswald as had been used when Oswald was brought into the station on 22 November.

TC - Page 215

Q. What was the American Civil Liberties Union's comment regarding Oswald's treatment while in custody?

A. On 6 December 1963 the ACLU commented "It is our opinion that Lee Harvey Oswald, had he lived, would have been deprived of all opportunity to receive a fair trial by the conduct of the police and prosecuting officials in Dallas, under pressure from the public and news media."

"From the moment of his arrest until his murder two days later, Oswald was tried and convicted many times over in the newspapers, on the radio, and over television by the public statements of the Dallas law enforcement officials. Time and again high-ranking police and prosecution officials state their complete satisfaction that Oswald was the assassin. As their investigation uncovered one piece of evidence after another, the results were broadcast to the public."

"...Oswald's trial would...have been nothing but a hollow formality."

PD - Page 349

Q. Was Police Chief Jesse Curry present in the basement when Oswald was killed?

A. No. Reportedly he received a telephone call from Mayor Earle Cabell just as he was leaving to supervise the transfer of Oswald. He said Cabell kept him on the telephone until Ruby shot Oswald.

HT - Page 285

Q. Did someone signal Ruby when Oswald was being transferred?

A. Yes. The only vehicles in the basement belonged to the police. At the moment Oswald came into view a horn sounded and then sounded again right before Ruby rushed forward and shot Oswald.

RTJ - Page 216

Q. What did the memo (dated 25 November 1963) Bill Moyers received from Deputy Attorney General Katzenbach say?

A. "It is important that all the facts surrounding President Kennedy's assassination be made public in a way which will satisfy people in the United States and abroad that all the facts have been told and that a statement to this effect be made now.

1. The public must be satisfied that Oswald was the assassin; that he did not have confederates who are still at large; and that the evidence was such that he could have been convicted at trial.

2. Speculation about Oswald's motivation ought to be cut off, and we should have some basis for rebutting thought that this was a Communist conspiracy or (as the Iron Curtain press is saying) a right-wing conspiracy to blame it on the Communists. Unfortunately, the facts on Oswald seem too pat -- too obvious (Marxist, Cuban, Russian wife, etc). The Dallas police have put out statements on the Community conspiracy theory, and it was they who were in charge when he was shot and silenced.

3. The matter has been handled thus far with neither dignity nor conviction. Facts have been mixed with rumor and speculation. We can scarcely let the world see us totally in the image of the Dallas police when our President is murdered. I think this objective may be satisfied by making public as soon as possible a complete and thorough FBI report on Oswald and the assassination. This may run into the difficulty of pointing to inconsistencies between this report and statements by Dallas police officials. But the reputation of the Bureau is such that it may well do the whole job".

HT - Page 257

Q. Was Marina Oswald ever held by Federal authorities?

A. Immediately after the assassination she said "Lee good man. Lee not shoot anyone". After being held by federal authorities for several weeks she testified that he was guilty.

CF - Page 129
HT - Page 158
PD - Page 344

Q. Was Marina Oswald concerned about being deported?

A. Yes. Today she says she was forced into her testimony by threats of deportation. According to authors Groden and Livingstone she would have testified to anything to avoid deportation.

HT - Page 209
PD - Page 344

Q. Which Federal agency held her?

A. Reportedly she was hidden by the Secret Service prior to her husband's murder, the purpose being to keep other government agencies from having access to her.

HT - Page 158
PD - Page 343

Q. Did the Secret Service help Marina Oswald after the assassination?

A. It has been documented that they helped arrange for her to hire James Martin, an employee of the Wynne-McKenzie law firm, as her business manager.

AOT - Page 498
HT - Page 283

Q. Did anyone coach Marina regarding her testimony?

A. Reportedly she was coached by her attorney William A. McKenzie, who had been a law partner of Bedford Wynne.

HT - Page 284

Q. Does Marina Oswald think Lee was guilty?

A. No. She believes that he worked for the American government and was killed so he couldn't reveal anything he knew.

CF - Page 129

Q. Was any evidence on Oswald destroyed by the FBI?

A. Yes. It is reported that a letter from Oswald to the FBI was ordered destroyed by Dallas FBI Agent-in-Charge Gordon Shanklin. There are varying stories regarding the content of the letter.

C - Pages 62, 63 & 361
FH - Page 70

Q. Did the Dallas police find a camera in Oswald's effects?

A. Yes, a small Minox "spy" camera, one which was not available to the public in 1963. The FBI tried to get the Dallas detectives to change their report, they refused. On the FBI property inventory it was listed as a "Minox light meter".

CF - Page 190

Q. Were any secret investigations of Oswald conducted after the assassination?

A. A former Marine navigator named Larry Huff told the House Assassinations Committee that he had taken part in a military investigation run out of Camp Smith, Hawaii. No reports of that investigation have been found.

HT - Page 273

Q. Were there any similarities between the diaries of Lee Oswald, Arthur Brehmer (who shot Governor George Wallace in 1972) and that of Sirhan-Sirhan (the alleged assassin of Robert Kennedy).

A. Yes, reportedly there are several similarities in style between all three, implying that they might all have been forgeries.

HT - Page 120

Q. Was Oswald's diary a fake?

A. The House Assassinations Committee concluded the diary was a forgery done in Russia. They were told by handwriting experts that the entire diary was written by Oswald in one or two sittings using the same kind of paper.

HT - Page 120
SS - Page 137

Q. What did former Dallas Police Chief Jesse Curry tell reporter Tom Johnson?

A. He said that he did not think Oswald acted alone. "We don't have any proof that Oswald fired the rifle, and never did. Nobody's yet been able to put him in that building with a gun in his hand".

HT - Page 237

Q. Did President Johnson ever express an opinion regarding Oswald?

A. Yes. In 1969 he referred to Oswald as "quite a mysterious fellow, and he did have connections that bore examination". A May 14, 1976 article in the San Francisco Examiner said

"Re-opening of the investigation recalled a belief of President Johnson that Oswald did not act alone. Johnson told interviewers he believed that Kennedy was killed in retaliation for a thwarted assassination attempt by a CIA-backed team of killers in Havana."

C - Page 101
HT - Page 344

Q. What were Senator Gary Hart's conclusions regarding Oswald?

A. In 1976 Senator Hart was appointed (along with Senator Richard Schweiker) by the Senate Intelligence Committee to study the responses of the FBI and CIA to the President's assassination, and Oswald's actual role. They had access to classified files. Senator Hart's comment was, "I don't think you can see the things I have seen and sit on it...knowing what I know -- I can't walk away from it." He wanted a further investigation into "who Oswald really was -- who did he know? What affiliation did he have in the Cuban network? Was his public identification with the left a cover for a connection with the anti-Castro right wing?" He felt that Oswald could not have acted as a double agent.

C - Page 265

Q. What did Senator Richard Russell say about the assassination?

A. He believed there had been a conspiracy, that there was more than one gunman and that "we have not been told the truth about Oswald".

HT - Page 67

Q. What did Gerald Ford later say about Oswald?

A. Former President Ford admitted that the Warren Commission never was able to find a motive for Oswald's alleged crimes.

AOT - Page 431

Q. Actor Peter Lawford was President Kennedy's brother-in-law. Did he believe in Oswald's guilt?

A. No. When asked if Oswald killed the President or if it was higher up he said, "it was higher up".

PL - Page 351

Q. Was Oswald's body ever exhumed?

A. Yes, on 4 October 1981. The doctors identified the body as Oswald's. However, weeks later the two funeral directors who had prepared Oswald's body for burial said that the body exhumed in 1981 was not the one they buried in 1963. The Oswald they buried had a craniotomy during the autopsy. They saw no sign of this on the skull they saw in 1981.

CF - Page 551
HT - Page 343

Q. Should Lee Harvey Oswald's name be on the list of dead witnesses?

A. Yes. Many researchers believe that he was never meant to be arrested. That the intent was to kill him before he could leave the book depository. When he got away, they think he was supposed to have been killed in the alley behind the Texas Theater. According to Sam Giancana, J.D. Tippit was supposed to have killed Oswald.

DC - Page 330, 335
HT - Page 131

The Manipulator

Q. Who was Jack Ruby?

A. His real name was Jack Rubenstein. He was a runner for Al Capone in Chicago in his early years, and in later years he continued to have ties to organized crime as well as the Teamsters Union. He was allegedly the owner of The Carousel Club, a Dallas striptease joint.

CF - Page 387
DC - Page 329
HT - Page 282 & 295

Q. What were Jack Ruby's ties to Richard Nixon?

A. FBI documentation shows that in 1947 Jack Rubenstein (alias Jack Ruby) of Chicago was acting as an informant for Congressman Richard Nixon. He was not called to testify before the House Committee on Un-American Activities because of this connection.

CF - Page 269
DC - Page 287
HT - Page 295

Q. What were Jack Ruby's ties to the FBI?

A. Reportedly Ruby contacted the FBI early in 1959 and volunteered to be an informant. Records indicate that he met with agents of the Bureau at least eight times that year.

CF - Page 235
FH - Page 316

Q. Was there anything unusual about Jack Ruby's telephone bills prior to the assassination?

A. Yes. According to researchers the bills for the weeks and hours before the assassination showed that he had been calling members of organized crime.

FH - Pages 94 & 324
HT - Page 413

Q. Did Jack Ruby have financial problems?

A. Yes. He had failed to file income tax returns and the IRS had issued tax liens which reportedly were over $40,000.

AOT - Page 278
HT - Page 280
RC - Page 55

Q. Was there a connection between Jack Ruby and the Hunt family of Dallas?

A. Yes. The name of one of H.L. Hunt's sons was found in Ruby's notebook and Ruby was in the Hunt offices the day before the assassination.

CF - Page 337
TC - Page 250

Q. Did Jack Ruby and J.D. Tippit know each other?

A. It has been documented that Tippit frequently visited Ruby's night club and they appeared to be close friends.

AOT - Page 261

Q. Did Oswald and Ruby know each other?

A. According to several people including General Edwin A. Walker, Ruby and Oswald did know each other and were seen in each other's company.

CF - Page 403
DC - Page 332
FH - Page 39

Q. Where was Jack Ruby when Oswald was arrested??

A. Eyewitness George J. Applin reported that he saw Ruby in the Texas Theater at the time of Oswald's arrest.

CF - Page 352

Q. Was Jack Ruby friendly with the Dallas Police Department?

A. Yes. He was a frequent visitor and members of the Police Department were always welcome in his club.

DC - Page 330

215

Q. Did Jack Ruby try to get into Captain Fritz's office.

A. It appears Jack Ruby was free to wander all over police headquarters and he was seen by a television reporter named Vic Robertson, Jr. trying to open the door of Captain Fritz's office while Oswald was being questioned.

AOT - Page 412

Q. How did Ruby prepare himself for the shooting of Oswald?

A. He told reporter Tom Johnson that he had taken 30 antibiotic and "dexidrene" pills to stimulate himself.

HT - Page 237

Q. Who was Jack Ruby's attorney and where was he at the time Oswald was shot?

A. His name was Tom Howard and he was reportedly in the basement near Ruby ready to provide legal counsel.

HT - Page 137

216

Q. What were Ruby's comments when he was arrested?

A. "I had to do it, because they (the police) weren't going to do it."

Q. Why was Jack Ruby always held in the Dallas County Jail instead of a Federal facility?

A. He had killed the accused assassin of the President of the United States but it was not a Federal offence in 1963 to kill the President. There may have been other reasons as well.

RD - Page 15

Q. Was Jack Ruby ever given a lie-detector or "truth-serum" test?

A. Reportedly he volunteered to take either test but Hoover refused to allow them on the grounds that they were "unreliable".

AOT - Page 456

Q. Did Jack Ruby ever ask to be taken to Washington, D.C.?

A. Yes. Eight times he asked Earl Warren to get him out of Dallas so that he could tell what really happened, but he never left Dallas alive.

C - Page 431
CF - Page 427
FH - Page 361
HT - Page 295 & 297
RD - Page 89

Q. Did Ruby ever accuse others of involvement in the assassination?

A. Yes, the Nazis and President Johnson.

CF - Page 430

Q. What was Ruby's reply when asked if the truth would ever be told?

A. In a taped interview, now available to the public, Ruby stated "No, because, unfortunately, these people who have so much to gain and have such an ulterior motive to put me in the position I'm in, will never let the true facts come above board to the world". This is an exact quote.

CF - Page 381
TC - Page 259

Q. Did Jack Ruby think someone was going to kill him?

A. Yes. He reportedly told members of the Warren Commission "I am used as a scapegoat...But if I am eliminated, there won't be any way of knowing."

HT - Page 297

Q. How did Jack Ruby die?

A. He was diagnosed as having lung cancer and died a short time later on 3 January 1967 in Parkland Hospital. He told family members he believed that he had been injected with cancer cells. Reportedly, the cancer cells found in Ruby's body were the type found in the digestive system, not the lungs.

CF - Page 433
HT - Page 298

Assassination Aftermath

Q. What did Chief Justice Earl Warren say about the assassination?

A. "You may never get the truth in your lifetime, and I mean that seriously."

PD - Page 53

Q. What was Executive Order 11625?

A. It sealed a large amount of evidence and documentation related to the assassination in the National Archives until the year 2039.

CF - Page 297

Q. Who signed Executive Order 11625?

A. President Johnson.

CF - Page 297

Q. Why didn't the Federal government have jurisdiction in the case?

A. In 1963 it was not a Federal crime to assassinate the President. It is now.

AOT - Page 533
CF - Page 150
HT - Page 266
RD - Page 15

Q. If the Federal government didn't have jurisdiction in the case, why was the FBI put in charge of the investigation?

A. They were put in charge by President Johnson.

CF - Pages 150 & 250
FH - Page 23
TC - Page 18

Q. Why wasn't the assassination investigated in Texas?

A. According to researcher Mary Ferrell, Captain Will Fritz received a call from the White House the day after the assassination telling him "You've got your man, the investigation is over."

HT - Pages 188 & 285

Q. What is the duty of the "bagman", who was he and what happened to him on 22 November 1963?

A. The "bagman" travels with the President at all times and carries a suitcase containing the device which could activate the nation's war machine. On 22 November, the "bagman" Major General Chester Clifton, was separated, first from President Kennedy and then from President Johnson, and was left behind at the airport in Dallas.

HT - Page 21

Q. Is there anything unusual about the locations of various prominent people around the time of the assassination?

A. Yes. Hardly any members of the administration were in Washington. The night of 21 November both J. Edgar Hoover and Richard Nixon were reportedly in Dallas at the home of oil magnate Clint Murchison. Six cabinet members and two Presidential aides, were on a plane headed for Japan. Vice President Johnson was in Texas with the President. When asked, within a few months of the assassination, where he was at the time, Nixon said he didn't remember.

CF - Page 267
DP - Page 89
HT - Pages 14, 20, 237, 282

Q. What was the so-called "Del Charro Set"?

A. According to authors Groden and Livingstone it was made up of Murchison & Wynne, millionaire Texas gamblers, and a group of their wealthy friends.

HT - Page 282

Q. What was J. Edgar Hoover's connection to the "Del Charro Set"?

A. Reportedly his annual holidays at the Del Mar racetrack in California were paid for by Murchison and Wynne.

AOT - Page 494
HT - Page 282

Q. Did President Eisenhower have any connections to the "Del Charro Set"?

A. They reportedly "bankrolled" his Gettysburg farm.

HT - Page 282

Q. What did leaders in the USSR do when they learned of the assassination?

A. They ordered a nuclear alert since they expected to be blamed for the President's death.

C - Page 532

Q. What did the Russian press say about the assassination?

A. They, too, concluded that there had been Mafia involvement.

AOT - Page 440

Q. What happened on the Stock Market on 22 November?

A. The Dow Jones made a startling drop -- the greatest panic since 1929 -- and the doors were closed 80 minutes early. Unidentified spectators made over $500 million in the early hours of 22 November suggesting that they had advance information regarding the assassination plan. Their names have never been revealed.

CF - Page 274
HT - Page 280

Q. How did the assassination of JFK differ from the other three Presidential assassinations and the six unsuccessful attempts?

A. In every instance except one, the assassins either stated the reason for their action or it was easily determined. The exception was the death of President Kennedy.

TC - Page 36

Q. What were the odds against 18 material witnesses in the Kennedy assassination being dead within 39 months?

A. *The London Sunday Times* concluded that on 22 November 1963 the odds would have been one hundred thousand trillion to one that all 18 would have died by February 1967.

CF - Page 555
RD - Page 412

Q. What was the Assassination Committee's chief researcher's response regarding deaths of witnesses?

A. Jacqueline Hess was quoted as saying "Our final conclusion on the issue is that the available evidence does not establish anything about the nature of these deaths which would indicate that the deaths were in some matter, either direct or peripheral, caused by the assassination of President Kennedy or by any aspect of the subsequent investigation."

HT - Page 129

Q. What was Henry Gonzalez' comment about the Assassinations Committee?

228

A. He felt the investigation was being sabotaged "because vast and powerful forces including the country's most sophisticated criminal element won't stand for it..." On 6 March 1977 he said that the Committee was "a put-up job and a hideous farce that was never intended to work...there's something very strange going on in this country--strange and frightening".

HT - Page 363

Q. Was Fidel Castro involved in the assassination?

A. He has been quoted as saying that only an insane person would plan the death of a United States President, and that the leaders of the Cuban Revolution wouldn't have had that sort of madness.

C - Pages 264, 411 & 412

Q. Did Fidel Castro have any theories regarding the assassination?

A. Yes. He said "I am under the impression that Kennedy's assassination was organized by some reactionaries in the United States.

C - Page 414

Q. Did anyone suddenly come into money after the assassination?

A. Yes. George DeMohrenschildt's* bank account in Port-au-Prince, Haiti reportedly received a deposit of over $200,000. Jack Ruby who owed the IRS in excess of $40,000 is said to have had $7,000 in cash on the afternoon of the assassination. Oswald's brother Robert reportedly received $25,000.

HT - Page 279, 281 and 302

Q. Who were the members of the Warren Commission?

A. Earl Warren, Chief Justice of the Supreme Court, Hale Boggs, Representative from Louisiana, John Sherman Cooper, Senator from Kentucky, Allen Dulles, former CIA Director (fired by JFK), Gerald Ford, Representative from Michigan, Richard Russell, Senator from Georgia, and John J. McCloy, a banker.

CF - Page 465
FH - Page 25

Q. How did Fletcher Prouty* describe the conspiracy?

A. It was a "domestic coup" rather than international involvement.

HT - Page 55

Q. Was the assassination a coup d'etat?

A.. Yes, according to many assassination experts including Larry Howard and Fletcher Prouty.

CF - Page 590
DC - Page 336

Q. What was Jim Garrison's definition of a coup d'etat?

A. It is "a sudden action by which an individual or group, usually employing limited violence, captures positions of governmental authority without conforming to the formal requirement for changing office holders, as prescribed by the laws or constitution." In his opinion the Kennedy assassination contained all the necessary ingredients for a successful coup.

OTT - Page 277

Q. Was the assassination a military-style ambush?

A. According to authors Robert Groden and Harrison Livingstone it had all the earmarks of one.

HT - Page 407

Q. Was anyone in the CIA concerned about Jim Garrison's assassination investigation?

A. Former CIA employee Victor Marchetti said Richard Helms was very concerned.

HT - Page 186
RD - Page 288

Q. Did anyone confirm that figures in the Garrison investigation were connected with the CIA?

A. Yes. According to Victor Marchetti, in 1969 CIA Director Richard Helms admitted that David Ferrie and Clay Shaw had worked for the CIA.

CF - Page 188

Q. Was Jim Garrison's investigation infiltrated by the CIA?

A. Yes. According to Jim Garrison he later found that many of the "volunteers" helping in the investigation actually had ties to the CIA.

OTT - Page 175

Q. Did Jim Garrison conclude that the CIA was involved in the assassination?

A. Yes. When he investigated the "key players" it became obvious to him. Guy Banister had ties to the Office of Naval Intelligence as well as the FBI and worked in New Orleans with anti-Castro Cubans who had to be CIA. David Ferrie had trained anti-Castro guerrillas for the Bay of Pigs invasion which we now know was a CIA operation. Garrison said "everything kept coming back to Cuba and the Bay of Pigs and the CIA".

OTT - Page 175

Q. Did anyone else state that the CIA was involved in the assassination?

A. Yes, reportedly Sam Giancana said that in the spring of 1963 he and his "CIA associates" were making final plans to kill the President.

DC - Page 333

Q. Did David Ferrie ever admit his involvement in the assassination?

A. He admitted to a friend that he had driven to Houston to meet a plane carrying two men from Dallas. The plane was to have been piloted by one of the assassins. Ferrie was to have flown them to a location farther away. He said the plane never arrived.

OTT - Page 120

Q. What did Former CIA Director Richard Helms tell the Assassinations Committee about Clay Shaw?

A. Helms said, "The only recollection I have of Clay Shaw and the Agency is that I believe that at one time as a businessman he was one of the part-time contacts of the Domestic Contact Division -- the people that talked to businessmen, professors, and so forth, and who travelled in and out of the country."

OTT - Page 251

Q. Did Clay Shaw take out a contract on Jim Garrison?

A. He reportedly offered Edward Whalen, a professional criminal from Philadelphia, $25,000 to kill Garrison.

CF- Page 502

Q. Where is Oak Cliff?

A. A suburb of Dallas, about five miles from Dealey Plaza, it was the home of Oswald, the site of the Texas Theater where he was arrested, and was where Dallas Police Officer J.D. Tippit was killed. It was also the location of Red Bird Airport.

Q. Was there a cover-up in Officer Tippit's murder?

A. Yes. Evidence was concealed, evidence disappeared and leads given by witnesses at the scene were never pursued.

OTT - Page 202

Q. How many bullets recovered from Tippit's body were sent to the FBI laboratory?

A. Of the four recovered three of them had been manufactured by Winchester Western, the fourth was manufactured by Remington-Peters. Only one of the four was sent to Washington.

OTT - Page 199
RD - Page 152

Q. Were FBI agents ordered to not investigate the Tippit murder?

A. Reportedly, J. Edgar Hoover ordered that the agents in Dallas not question witnesses at the scene.

OTT - Page 197

236

Q. What was the significance of Red Bird Airport?

A. Two days before the assassination three men went to the airport to reserve a plane to fly to Mexico on 22 November.

AOT - Page 369
CF - Page 355

Q. How many people were involved in the assassination?

A. Governor Connally told the Warren Commission there were three or more.

CF - Page 12

Q. Did any witnesses see more than one man on the sixth floor of the Texas School Book Depository?

A. Mr. and Mrs. Arnold Rowland saw two men, as did Deputy Sheriff Roger Craig. Two men can be seen in two films made that day.

CF - Page 20-22

Q. What did Marita Lorenz* tell author Mark Lane?

A. She said she travelled in a automobile with Frank Sturgis from Miami to Dallas in November 1963. She said that there were two cars with the second car carrying weapons and that once they checked into a motel in Dallas they were visited by both E. Howard Hunt and Jack Ruby. She told Lane that Sturgis, who was using the name Frank Fiorini, was given an envelope containing money by Hunt. She said the meeting was held on 21 November 1963. Once she realized what was going to happen she said she had Sturgis (Fiorini) take her to the airport and she flew back to New York City where she was when the assassination occurred.

PD - Page 296

Q. What did Marita Lorenz say she was told by Frank Sturgis after the assassination?

A. "We killed the President that day. You could have been a part of it -- you know, part of history. You should have stayed. It was safe. Everything was covered in advance. No arrests, no real newspaper investigation. It was all covered, very professional."

PD - Page 303

Q. Was Marita Lorenz ever questioned by the FBI?

A. Yes. She said she was questioned by them in New York in November following the assassination. She reportedly gave them all the information she knew.

PD - Page 302

Q. Did the FBI change testimony of witnesses?

A. According to Julia Ann Mercer, a witness who saw Jack Ruby near the Grassy Knoll, key portions of her statement were altered and her signature was forged.

CF - Page 481
HT - Pages 77, 268-270

Q. Were witnesses in Dallas deliberately silenced?

A. According to Groden and Livingstone witnesses were visited by "government" agents who either silenced them or told them what to say.

HT - Page 267

Q. Did the FBI intimidate any witnesses?

A. A report in The New York Times on 5 December 1963 stated "most private citizens who had cooperated with newsmen reporting the crime have refused to give further help after being interviewed by agents of the Federal Bureau of Investigation".

HT - Page 89

Q. Was any evidence ignored?

A. Many witnesses were never interviewed, evidence that the President was shot from the front in the face was ignored, as was evidence of a fusillade of shots from at least three directions.

HT - Page 264

Q. Was evidence fabricated?

A. Many researchers believe so. For instance, neither the Dallas police or FBI found fingerprints or palm prints on the alleged murder weapon. Later the FBI received a palm print of Oswald's which was said to have been found on the rifle.

HT - Page 268

Q. Who was the "umbrella man"?

A. One of two men seen on Elm Street close to the time JFK was shot. One researcher theorized that the umbrella may have been a weapon which fired a paralyzing dart into the President. The CIA had such a weapon in 1963.

CF - Page 30

Q. Was Charles Cabell* still involved with the CIA at the time of the President's death?

A. Yes, he was on the board of Air America which was a CIA operation.

HT - Page 314

Q. Did someone have a seizure near the Texas School Book Depository before the shooting?

A. Yes. Reportedly a young man wearing Army fatigues collapsed near the front door of the Texas School Book Depository shortly before the motorcade was due. An ambulance was dispatched from Parkland Hospital but there is no record of his having been treated. Some felt that the incident was planned to distract attention from the shooting.

CF - Page 42
OTT - Page 96

Q. Was evidence in the Presidential limousine destroyed?

A. Yes, the Secret Service washed away bullet fragments with buckets of water on the same day as the assassination.

HT - Page 73 & 74
OTT - Page 222

Q. Was anyone allowed to photograph the inside of the limousine in Dallas?

A. Texas Department of Public Safety Officer Hurchel Jacks stated on 28 November 1963 that he had been assigned by the Secret Service to prevent any photographs being taken of the limousine's interior.

HT - Page 86

Q. What happened to the limousine after the assassination?

A. Reportedly within 48 hours it was taken to Detroit and completely dismantled, thus destroying vital evidence.

CF - Page 450
TC - Page 254

Q. Were the American people allowed to see the Zapruder film right after the assassination?

A. No. Not for more than ten years. Some frames of the film were printed in the Warren Report but the two frames showing the head shot were in reverse order.

C - Page 31

Q. Were any reporters allowed to see the Zapruder film?

A. Yes, Dan Rather. He described the film over nationwide radio and stated that the President's head "went forward with considerable violence."

CF - Page 68

Q. Why were the still photographs made from frames in the Zapruder film transposed in the Warren Report?

A. To support the lone gunman theory. By transposing the frames, the President's head appears to have been thrown forward by the bullet's impact instead of rearward which was what actually happened. J. Edgar Hoover explained the reversal as a "printing error".

CF - Page 67

Q. In what way was the Zapruder film changed?

A. Researchers who examined the original film stated that it had been spliced, frames appeared to have been retouched and otherwise tampered with.

CF - Page 69
HTII - Page 447

Q. What was the result of a Gallup Poll taken the first week of December 1963?

A. Fifty-two percent of those polled believed that Oswald had not acted alone.

CF - Page 461

Q. What were the results of a Gallup Poll taken in 1976?

A. That 80% of Americans believed that Oswald had not acted alone.

HT - Page 357

Q. What did President Johnson later tell Marvin Watson?

A. That he "was convinced that there was a plot in connection with the assassination and that the CIA had something to do with this plot."

PD - Page 109

Q. Who was John Stockwell and what were his conclusions regarding the assassination?

A. He was an intelligence officer who served on a subcommittee of the National Security Council. He concluded that Florida-based CIA operatives had organized the assassination and used anti-Castro Cuban exiles to carry it out.

PD - Page 111

Q. Are the assassins still alive?

A. Researchers Robert Groden and Harrison Livingstone believe they are. They say a more important point is that the persons who ordered and organized the assassination are still alive.

DC - Page 357
HT - Page 424

Q. What happened when President Carter tried to discuss the assassination on live television?

A. There was no televised sound for almost half an hour.

HT - Page 417

Q. What has happened to prominent people involved in the assassination investigation?

A. Arlen Specter, who along with Gerald Ford developed the "magic bullet theory", became a U.S. Senator from Pennsylvania. Ford became President after Nixon's resignation but was not re-elected. Marina Oswald was hidden by the Secret Service in a motel owned by the Great Southwest Corporation which the Wynne family of Dallas controlled. The Wynnes were partners of Clint Murchison, who had J.Edgar Hoover and Richard Nixon as guests at his home the night before the assassination. Murchison, according to researchers, received large loans from the Teamster's pension fund. President Ford ordered that intelligence activities be investigated by Vice President Nelson Rockefeller. In the midst of this "whitewashed" investigation it was revealed that there may have been a tie-in between the assassination and Watergate.

HT - Page 281

Q. What was on the 18-minute gap which was erased from the Watergate tapes?

A. It was a discussion about President Kennedy's assassination.

HT - Page 331

Q. What was Operation Chaos?

A. We are told it was a CIA operation run by James Angleton* and included illegal mail openings and surveillance against private citizens during Nixon's term in office.

HT - Page 358

Q. Did Richard Nixon ever travel to Cuba?

A. Yes. According to biographer Earl Mazo, Nixon visited Cuba in 1940 checking on the possibility of establishing business connections or a law practice in Havana.

CF - Page 169

Q. Did Richard Nixon have any Mafia connections?

A. It has been reported that his close friend and campaign manager Murray Chotiner was an attorney who represented leading mobsters and had connections to Carlos Marcello of New Orleans and Jimmy Hoffa. Mobster Mickey Cohen wrote that he gave $5,000 for Nixon's 1946 congressional campaign.

CF - Page 268
DC - Page 286
HT - Pages 293, 294, 317

Q. Did Richard Nixon have Mafia backing for his 1960 Presidential campaign?

A. Yes. It has been documented by several researchers that he was given a campaign contribution by Carlos Marcello in the amount of $500,000 in cash.

CF - Page 268
DC - Page 286
MK

Q. What was the message delivered to Richard Helms by H.R. Haldeman?

A. According to Nixon aide H.R. Haldeman, after the Watergate break-in Nixon wanted the CIA's help in the cover-up. Haldeman said he told Helms "the President asked me to tell you this entire affair may be connected to the Bay of Pigs and if it blows up, the Bay of Pigs may be blown..." Haldeman also said that "It seems that in all of those Nixon references to the Bay of Pigs he was actually referring to the Kennedy assassination."

PD - Page 110

Q. Where did Richard Nixon make his first public appearance after his resignation?

A. He was seen at La Costa, a retreat near San Clemente which was frequented by the Mafia and Earl Warren. With Nixon were Teamsters President Fitzsimmons, Tony Provenzano who had Mafia ties, Jack Presser and Allen Dorfman, both representatives of the Teamsters Union. One of La Costa's founders was Jim Braden* who was arrested in Dallas minutes after the assassination.

HT - Page 318

The Warren Commmission

Q. Who ordered the formation of the Warren Commission?

A. President Johnson.

Q. What seems to have been the motivation behind the Warren Report?

A. According to authors Groden and Livingstone it appears to have been politically motivated by individuals with knowledge that evidence of a conspiracy within their own organizations existed. Warren Commission member John J. McCloy was quoted at saying on 5 December 1963 "I have a feeling that we have another obligation than the mere evaluation of the reports of agencies, many of which as you suggested, or some of them at least, may be interested, may be involved". This is a direct quote.

HT - Page 263

Q. What was the first book to openly challenge the Warren Report?

A. It was *Rush To Judgement* by Mark Lane, published in 1966.

Q. Were there attempts to disbar Mark Lane after he wrote *Rush To Judgement*?

A. Yes. According to Lane, Lewis F. Powell, Jr. who later became a United States Supreme Court justice suggested that Lane be disbarred and proceedings were begun in New York City. Apparently the charge was later withdrawn but Lane says he has never been notified of that fact.

PD - Page 24

Q. Did any government agencies try to keep American publishers from printing *Rush To Judgement*?

A. Yes. Lane had the book published in England when he was unable to find a publisher in the United States. Years later he learned that the CIA and FBI had exerted pressure to block its publication.

PD - Page 25

Q. What did Senator Richard Schweiker say about the Warren Commission?

A. He was quoted as saying "I think the Warren Commission has, in fact, collapsed like a house of cards. And I believe the Warren Commission was set up at a time to feed pablum to the American people for reasons not yet known, and that one of the biggest cover-ups in the history of our country occurred at that time.

CF - Page 491

Q. Were members of the Warren Commission allowed to see all the evidence?

A. No. Evidence was withheld from them by the FBI, Secret Service and CIA.

FH - Page 84
HT - Page 85

Q. Did the FBI suppress evidence regarding the assassination?

A. Yes. During the fall of 1963, Jack Ruby met with mob figure Johnny Roselli on two different occasions. This information was not given to the Warren Commission.

CF - Page 401

Q. Did the Secret Service turn over all the evidence they had to the Warren Commission?

A. No, and much of that evidence has since disappeared.

HT - Page 263

Q. What does former Warren Commission counsel Burton Griffin say now about the FBI & CIA?

A. He has been quoted as saying "What is most disturbing to me is that two agencies of the government, that were supposed to be loyal and faithful to us, deliberately misled us."

C - Page 532

Q. Did a member of the Warren Commission leak information to the FBI?

A. Yes. Gerald Ford allegedly passed classified information to Hoover's assistant Cartha DeLoach and reportedly told DeLoach to "call him anytime his assistance was needed".

AOT - Page 397
FH - Page 86
PD - Page 43

Q. What are "raw" files?

A. Files which have not been edited.

Q. Did the Warren Commission ever demand "raw" FBI files?

A. Yes, on 16 December 1963 they made a public demand for files from Hoover. Hoover reportedly was furious but could not refuse.

AOT - Page 393, 483

Q. Were CIA employees "coached" regarding their testimony before the Warren Commission?

A. Yes. They were reportedly programmed by Warren Commission member and former CIA Director Allen Dulles.

SS - Page 132

Q. Were all of the assassination witnesses called to testify before the Warren Commission?

A. No. Many, including eyewitnesses and law officers who were at the scene, were never allowed to appear.

C - Page 22
HT - Page 264

Q. How many witnesses were questioned by the Warren Commission?

A. Only 126 of the known 266 witnesses, less than one half, gave testimony.

CF - Page 435

Q. Were witnesses questioned about the direction from which the shots came?

A. Most were not. Of those who were, thirty-two said they came from the Texas School Book Depository, thirty-eight gave no opinion, fifty-one indicated they came from the area near the Grassy Knoll. Several believed there was gunfire from two directions.

CF - Page 435

Q. Was any information regarding people shooting from the Grassy Knoll omitted from the Warren Report?

A. Yes, including the testimony of Jean Hill, Gayle Newman and William Newman.

C - Page 23

Q. Did anyone threaten eyewitness Jean Hill?

A. Yes. According to Ms. Hill, Warren Commission attorney Arlen Specter told her she could be admitted to a mental hospital if she didn't cooperate with the Commission.

258

CF - Page 484

Q. Did the Warren Commission change the testimony of some of the witnesses?

A. Eyewitness Sam Holland said he and his attorney attempted to correct his testimony but his changes never appeared in the final report.

CF - Page 480

Q. Were any of the civilian photographers in Dealey Plaza called on to testify?

A. No.

CF - Page 481

Q. Did William Greer, driver of the Presidential limousine, give false testimony?

A. Yes. He testified before the Warren Commission that he accelerated when Agent Roy Kellerman yelled, "Get out of here, fast." The Nix film, taken at the time, shows the brake lights were on until after the fatal headshot was fired. Only then did he accelerate.

CF - Page 245

Q. What was the "magic bullet"?

A. This was the theory developed by the Warren Commission to prove there was only one gunman and that President Kennedy and Governor Connally were both wounded with the same bullet.

C - Page 34
OTT - Page 240

Q. Could the magic bullet theory be correct?

A. Not according to extensive evidence including the Zapruder film, eyewitnesses, and especially Governor and Mrs. Connally. Over half the members of the Warren Commission never accepted the "magic bullet" theory.

C - Pages 35-39
HT - Pages 63-70, & 373
RD - Page 63-70

Q. What is a "pristine bullet"?

A. It is a bullet which shows little or no damage such as the one found on a stretcher at Parkland Hospital.

Q. Is the "pristine bullet" now used as evidence the actual one found on the stretcher at Parkland Hospital?

A. Not according to Darrell Tomlinson who found the original bullet. He said the one he found looked completely different from the one identified as CE399.

HT - Page 118

Q. Who placed the "pristine bullet" on that stretcher at Parkland Hospital?

A. Several reports indicate that it was planted by Jack Ruby who was identified at the scene by reporter Seth Kantor.

HT - Page 118
RC - Page 8

Q. Did Governor Connally believe there was only one gunman?

A. No. He felt there were two or more people firing or else
someone shooting an automatic rifle.

C - Page 19
CF - Page 112

The Nemesis

Q. Why was J. Edgar Hoover* one of the most feared men in Washington?

A. His deputy director, William Sullivan*, said Hoover was the "greatest blackmailer of all time". His personal files filled four rooms at the FBI Building. Reportedly, the files were destroyed after Hoover's death.

CF - Page 222
MK - Page 259

Q. What was in Hoover's directive on 24 November 1963?

A. He sent a message to ex-agent and Dallas district attorney Henry Wade who then called a press conference and announced that Oswald was the sole assassin and the case was closed.

AOT - Page 393

Q. What did the European press say about Hoover on 27 November 1963?

A. They suggested that Jack Ruby had mob backing and they accused Hoover of complicity in the assassination.

AOT - Page 404

Q. What were Hoover's conclusions regarding the assassination?

A. On 5 December 1963 he publicly stated that Oswald and Ruby acted alone and independent of one another and demanded that the newly-formed Warren Commission issue a statement in agreement with him.

AOT - Page 14

Q. Did J. Edgar Hoover want the assassination investigated fully?

A. No. He objected to the formation of the Warren commission and wanted the case closed. Hours after the assassination he stated that there was no conspiracy and that Lee Harvey Oswald acted alone. He blocked the Warren Commission's investigation at every opportunity. The FBI's position has continued to be that Oswald acted alone.

AOT
C - Pages 417-436
FH - Page 27
HT -Page 290
RD - Page 26

Q. Was Hoover involved in the assassination?

A. Author Mark North says that Hoover found out about a plot to kill President Kennedy in September 1962 but did nothing to prevent it.

AOT
CF - Page 240
HT - Page 309

Q. How did Hoover know so much about Oswald?

A. Hoover called Attorney General Robert Kennedy within two hours after the death of President Kennedy saying that he thought the killer was in custody and gave a background description of Oswald. How he had this information at his fingertips may never be known.

CF - Page 355

Q. Did J. Edgar Hoover conduct a vendetta against Dallas Police Chief Curry?

A. Yes. Chief Curry announced to newsmen that the FBI had withheld information on Oswald from the Dallas police. Until Curry retired in 1966, Hoover ordered that training courses not be conducted for Dallas police. Policemen from Dallas were not invited to the FBI Academy.

AOT - Page 393
CF - Page 219

Q. Was J. Edgar Hoover ever charged with obstruction of justice?

A. According to author Mark North he was "essentially" charged with obstruction of justice in January 1964 by the Warren Commission for his reluctance to provide them with the requested evidence.

AOT - Page 398

Q. Did Hoover ever perjure himself before the Warren Commission?

A. Reportedly on 14 May 1964 he stated that the FBI had never withheld data regarding threats on President Kennedy's life from the Secret Service. Documentation now proves that he lied.

AOT - Page 400

Q. Did Hoover have David Ferrie* and Carlos Marcello* investigated fully?

A. No. He had his agents stop their investigation of Ferrie on 18 December and no mention was made of either man in the FBI supplemental report on 13 January 1964.

AOT - Page 487

Q. What did Hale Boggs say about the FBI?

A. He publicly charged the FBI with using Gestapo tactics and alleged that the Bureau had wiretapped his telephone and telephones of other Congressmen as well. As a possible threat Congressman Boggs had been given "damaging material" on the lives of critics of the Warren Report and the FBI's investigation of the assassination by Hoover shortly before his plane disappeared in Alaska.

HT - Page 134

Q. What did Hoover say about organized crime?

A. He insisted that there was no problem with organized crime in the United States.

HT - Page 416

Q. Did Hoover ever admit Oswald had been innocent?

A. According to author, Mark North there was overwhelming evidence that Oswald was innocent, a fact that Hoover admitted in a memo on 24 November 1963.

AOT - Page 405

What Happened To Them?

In the three years immediately following the assassination of President Kennedy eighteen material witnesses died -- six by gunfire, three by motor accidents, three by "heart attacks", two by "suicide", two by "natural causes", one from a karate chop to the neck, and one from a slit throat. There would be more deaths occurring around the time of each subsequent investigation.

Who was --

Q. Karyn Kupcinet?

A. She was the daughter of a TV host who was overheard discussing the assassination before it happened. She was murdered on 24 November 1963.

CF - Page 558
HT - Page 141

Warren Commission

Q. Jack Zangretti?

A. He said Ruby was going to kill Oswald before it happened. He was shot and killed in December 1963.

CF - Page 558

Q. Eddy Benavides?

A. His look-alike brother, Domingo, was a witness to the Tippit shooting. He died from a gunshot to the head in February 1964.

CF - Page 558
HT - Page 143

Q. Betty MacDonald?

A. She had been an employee of Jack Ruby's at the Carousel Club in Dallas and was once at a private party with the Oswalds and DeMohrenschildts. She provided an alibi for

Darrell Wayne Garner and her testimony freed him in the shooting of Warren Reynolds. She was arrested in February 1964, one week after the not-guilty verdict and an hour later was found hanged in her jail cell.

CF - Page 558
HT - Page 138

Q. Bill Chesher?

A. He was thought to have evidence connecting Ruby and Oswald. He died of an apparent heart attack in March 1964.

CF - Page 558
HT - Page 135

Q. Hank Killam?

A. He was the husband of Ruby employee Wanda Joyce. Joyce had known Ruby since he moved to Dallas in 1947 and was also acquainted with John Carter who lived at 1026 North Beckley Avenue while Oswald also lived there. Killam told his brother "I'm a dead man, but have run as far as I am going to run". His throat was cut in March 1964.

CF - Page 558
HT - page 138

Q. Bill Hunter?

A. He was a reporter who had been at Ruby's apartment the night Ruby shot Oswald. He was shot and killed by a policeman in a Long Beach, California police station on 24 April 1964.

CF - Page 558
HT - Page 137

Q. Gary Underhill?

A. He was a former CIA intelligence operative who claimed Agency involvement in the assassination. He was found dead of a gunshot wound in the left side of the head in May 1964. His death was ruled a suicide. Underhill was right-handed.

CF - Page 559
HT - Page 144

Q. Hugh Ward?

A. He was a private investigator and a partner of Guy Banister and worked with David Ferrie as well. He died when a plane he was flying crashed in Mexico in May 1964.

CF - Page 559
HT - Page 144

Q. DeLesseps Morrison?

A. He was the Mayor of New Orleans and died in the plane crash with Hugh Ward.

CF - Page 559
HT - Page 144

Q. Teresa Norton?

A. She was one of Jack Ruby's strippers and a police inform-ant. She was shot to death in Houston in August 1964.

CF - Page 559
HT - Page 139

Q. Guy Banister?

A. He was a former FBI agent who ran a detective agency in New Orleans and was connected to David Ferrie, Carlos Marcello, Lee Oswald and the CIA. He reportedly died of a heart attack in June 1964, but some have said there was a bullet hole in his body.

C - Page 489
CF - Page 559
HT - Page 144

Q. Jim Koethe?

A. He was a reporter who also was in Ruby's apartment the night of 24 November 1963. A karate chop to the neck as he stepped out of the shower in his Dallas apartment killed him on 21 September 1964.

CF - Page 559
HT - Page 137

Q. C.D. Jackson?

A. He was the senior vice-president of Life magazine responsible for buying the Zapruder film and keeping it from the public. He died of "unknown causes" in September 1964.

CF - Page 559

Q. Mary Pinchot Meyer?

A. She was a mistress of JFK and was shot to death while jogging in October 1964. Her diary was allegedly taken by the CIA after her death.

CF - Page 559
PP - Page 64

Q. Paul Mandal?

A. He was a writer for Life magazine who said JFK was shot in the throat while turning to the rear. He died of "cancer" in January 1965.

CF - Page 559

Q. Tom Howard?

A. He was Jack Ruby's first attorney. Ruby said Howard told him to say he had shot Oswald so Jackie Kennedy would not have to return to Dallas to testify. Howard died of an apparent heart attack on 27 March 1965.

CF - Page 559

Q. Maurice Gatlin?

A. He was Guy Banister's pilot, had CIA involvement and acted as legal counsel for the Anti-Communist League of the Caribbean. He died in Panama in May 1965 when he fell or was pushed from a window.

CF - Page 559
HT - Page 145

Q. Mona Saenz?

A. She was a clerk with the Texas Employment Commission who interviewed Oswald. She was hit and killed by a Dallas bus in August 1965.

CF - Page 559

Q. David Goldstein?

A. He helped the FBI trace the pistol allegedly used in the murder of Officer Tippit. He died of "natural causes" in 1965.

CF - Page 559
HT - Page 137

Q. Rose Cheramie?

A. She was a prostitute and drug addict who had prior knowledge of the assassination and tried unsuccessfully to warn authorities. She was run over by a car and killed in September 1965.

CF - Page 559
HT - Page 141
RD - Page 412

Q. Dorothy Kilgallen?

A. She was a newspaper columnist who attended Jack Ruby's trial and had the only private interview with him. She died on 8 November 1965 reportedly of an overdose of barbiturates and alcohol. Five days before her death she had told a friend she was going to New Orleans to break the case wide open.

CF - Page 559
HT - Page 138

Q. Mrs. Earl Smith?

A. She was a close friend of Dorothy Kilgallen and may have kept the notes Kilgallen had on the case. She died of "unknown causes" two days after the columnist.

CF - Page 560
HT - Page 138

Q. William Whaley?

A. He was the cabdriver who reportedly drove Oswald to Oak Cliff after the assassination. He died in a freak car accident in December 1965, the first driver to be killed on duty since 1937.

CF - Page 560
HT - Page 139

Q. Judge Joe Brown?

A. He was the judge at Ruby's trial. Ruby's attorneys tried unsuccessfully to have Brown removed from the case after learning that Brown was negotiating a book deal on Ruby. Brown died of an apparent heart attack in 1966.

CF - Page 560

Q. Karen "Little Lynn" Carlin?

A. She was an employee of Jack Ruby to whom he wired money just before he shot Oswald. She was later shot to death in Houston.

CF - Page 560
HT - Page 139

Q. Earlene Roberts?

A. She was Lee Oswald's landlady who testified that while he was in her house following the assassination, a police car drove by and honked twice before moving slowly away. Mrs. Roberts died of heart failure on 9 January 1966.

CF - Page 560
HT - Page 139

Q. Albert Bogard?

A. He was an employee at the Downtown Dallas Lincoln-Mercury dealership who reported that, prior to the assassination Oswald test-drove a car on the Stemmons Freeway with Bogard as his passenger. Bogard was found dead in his car in a cemetery in Hallsville, Louisiana on 14 February 1966. One end of a hose was connected to the car's exhaust pipe and the other end was in the car with the windows rolled up. His death was ruled a suicide. Oswald did not drive.

CF - Page 560
HT - Page 132

Q. Captain Frank Martin?

A. He was a Dallas police captain who witnessed Oswald's murder and later told the Warren Commission "there's a lot to be said but probably be better if I don't say it." He died of cancer under questionable circumstances in June 1966.

CF - Page 560
HT - Page 141

Q. Lee Bowers, Jr.?

A. He was working in the railroad control tower behind the picket fence on the Grassy Knoll before the assassination. He reported having seen two men behind the fence and a puff of smoke during the shooting. Bowers was 41 when he died in a one-car crash 9 August 1966 near Midlothian, Texas. The Medical Examiner said Bowers was in some type of "strange shock" at the time of the accident.

CF - Page 560
HT - Page 135

Q. Marilyn "Delilah" Walle?

A. She was a stripper employed by Ruby who was planning a book on the assassination. She was shot to death 1 September

1966. Her husband was convicted of the crime. They had been married for only one month.

CF - Page 560
HT - Page 138

Q. William Pitzer?

A. He was a Navy Lt. Commander who filmed the Kennedy autopsy in detail. He was found shot to death on 29 October 1966 in his office at Bethesda Naval Hospital. His death was ruled a suicide and although an autopsy was performed, the results have never been released, even to his widow. He reportedly was very troubled by Kennedy's death. His family and friends remain convinced he was murdered.

CF - Page 560
HT - Pages 58 & 143

Q. Jimmy Levens?

A. He was a Fort Worth nightclub owner who hired some of Ruby's employees. He died of "natural causes" on 5 November 1966.

CF - Page 560
HT - Page 137

Q. James Worrell, Jr.?

A. He testified that he had seen a man run out the back door on the Texas School Book Depository and head south on Houston Street. He also said "I heard the fourth shot". He was 23 years old when he died in a car-motorcycle accident on 9 November 1966.

CF - Page 560
HT - Page 139

Q. Clarence Oliver?

A. He was an investigator for the District Attorney and worked on Jack Ruby's case. He died of "unknown causes" in 1966.

CF - Page 560

Q. Hank Suydam?

A. He was the Life Magazine official in charge of the JFK stories. He died of an apparent heart attack in December 1966.

CF - Page 560

Garrison's Investigation

Q. Leonard Pullin?

A. He was a civilian with the Navy who helped film "Last Two Days" about the assassination. He died in a one car accident in 1967.

CF - Page 561

Q. David Ferrie?

A. He was acquainted with Ruby, Oswald and Clay Shaw. He worked for Guy Banister as well as Carlos Marcello and was a CIA contract agent. He was Jim Garrison's star witness in his case against Shaw. He died of a questionable brain hemorrhage on 22 February 1967. Some researchers believe the cause of death was a blow to the neck. His death was ruled due to "natural causes".

C - Page 490
CF - Page 561
HT - Page 136

Q. Eladio del Valle?

A. A close friend of Ferrie, del Valle was an anti-Castro Cuban and reportedly an associate of Santos Trafficante. He was killed in Miami within the same hour Ferrie died in New Orleans. He had been shot in the heart at point-blank range and also had been struck in the head with a machete. Garrison had been trying to locate him for questioning at the time of his death.

CF - Page 561
HT - Page 136

Q. Dr. Mary Sherman?

A. She was another associate of David Ferrie and together they were working on cancer research. She died in March 1967 after being shot in bed and set on fire.

CF - Page 561
HT - Page 136

Q. A.D. Bowie?

A. He was an assistant Dallas District Attorney prosecuting Jack Ruby. He died of cancer in April 1968.

CF - Page 561

Q. Hiram Ingram?

A. He was a Dallas Sheriff and a close friend of Roger Craig who stated he had knowledge of a conspiracy in Kennedy's death. After falling and breaking his hip on 1 April 1968, he died three days later of "cancer".

CF - Page 561
HT - Page 141

Q. Dr. Nicholas Chetta?

A. He was the Coroner of New Orleans who ruled in the death of David Ferrie. He was also a key witness in Garrison's case against Shaw. He reportedly died of a heart attack on 25 May 1968.

287

CF - Page 561
HT - Page 135

Q. Philip Geraci?

A. He was a friend of Garrison witness Perry Russo and reportedly admitted hearing a conversation between Lee Oswald and Clay Shaw. He died of electrocution in August 1968.

CF - Page 561

Q. Henry Delaune?

A. He was the brother-in-law of, and sometime assisted, Dr. Nicholas Chetta. He was murdered 26 January 1969.

CF - Page 561
HT - Page 136

Q. E.R. "Buddy" Walthers?

A. He was a Dallas deputy sheriff who helped search the Texas School Book Depository. He reportedly found a .45

caliber slug in the grass beside Elm Street. He was shot and killed in a police shootout in 1969.

CF - Page 561
HT - Page 131

Q. Charles Mentesana?

A. He reportedly filmed a rifle other than the Mannlicher-Carcano being removed from the Texas School Book Depository. He died of a heart attack in 1969.

CF - Page 561

Q. John Crawford?

A. He was a close friend of both Jack Ruby and Wesley Frazier. He died in a mysterious plane crash in April 1969. *The Dallas Morning News* reported on 18 April 1969 that a radio was still playing in a trailer home when investigators arrived on the morning of the crash. They felt this was an indication that someone may have been in a hurry to leave. Another indication of a hurried departure was the position of the wheel blocks in the hangar where the plane had been stored. Six people died in the crash including the manager of the airport, another couple and their two children. The three cars left at the airport all had keys in their ignitions and the woman left her purse on the seat of one of them.

CF - Page 562
HT - Page 291

Q. Reverend Clyde Johnson?

A. He was beaten the day before he was due to testify at Clay Shaw's trial concerning the relationship between Shaw, Ferrie, Ruby, and Oswald. A short time later he was killed by a shotgun blast.

CF - Page 562
HT - Page 136

Q. George McGann?

A. He was an underworld figure and the husband of assassination witness Beverly Oliver. He was murdered in 1970 at the home of Ronny Weeden, and the murder has never been solved. Weeden knew Charles Harrelson in prison and Harrelson, the convicted killer of Federal Judge John Wood, says Weeden killed McGann. Weeden has since disappeared.

CF - Page 562
HT - Page 142

Q. Darrell Wayne Garner?

A. He was the prime suspect in the shooting of Warren Reynolds, but was released after being given an alibi by Betty MacDonald. He died of an apparent drug overdose in January 1970.

CF - Page 562

Q. Bill Decker?

A. He was the sheriff of Dallas who reported seeing bullets hit the street in front of the President's limousine. He died of "natural causes" in August 1970.

CF - Page 562

Q. Abraham Zapruder?

A. He was an amateur photographer who took the motion pictures of the assassination. He died of "natural causes" in August 1970.

CF - Page 562

Q. Salvatore Granello?

A. He was an underworld figure with links to Santos Trafficante, Jimmy Hoffa and the Castro assassination plots. He was shot and killed in December 1970.

C - Page 494
CF - Page 562

Q. James Plumeri?

A. He shared the same underworld ties as Granello and was also linked to mob-CIA assassination plots. He was murdered in 1971, a few months after Granello's death.

C - Page 494
CF - Page 562

Q. Clayton Fowler?

A. He was Jack Ruby's chief defense attorney. He died of unknown causes in March 1971.

CF - Page 562

Q. General Charles Cabell?

A. He was a former CIA deputy director who was fired by JFK after the Bay of Pigs disaster. He returned to Dallas where his brother was mayor and was living there at the time of the assassination. He collapsed and died in April 1971 after a routine physical examination at Fort Myers, Va.

CF - Page 562

Church Committee Investigation

Q. Hale Boggs?

A. He was a congressman from Louisiana, the House Majority leader and a member of the Warren Commission who began to publicly express his doubts about the findings of the Commission. He disappeared in July 1972 on a plane flight in Alaska shortly after publicly accusing the FBI of using Gestapo tactics, alleging that they had wiretapped his telephone.

CF - Page 562
HT - Page 134

Q. J. Edgar Hoover?

A. He was the Director of the FBI who pushed the theory that Lee Harvey Oswald was the lone assassin. He died suddenly in May 1972 at a critical time in his struggle with Richard Nixon and the CIA. According to authors Robert Groden and Harrison Livingstone, a report in the *Harvard Crimson* stated that the Senate's Ervin Committee was given evidence that Hoover's home had been broken into by a team led by Gordon Liddy and Cubans and that a poison which induces fatal heart attacks was placed on Hoover's toilet articles. No autopsy was performed.

HT - Page 420

Q. Thomas E. Davis?

294

A. He was a gunrunner connected with both the CIA and Jack Ruby. He was electrocuted by 7,000 volts when he cut into a power line he thought was disconnected. He was trying to steal copper wire at an abandoned rock-crusher in Wise County, Texas.

CF - Page 562

Q. Joseph Milteer?

A. He was described by an FBI informant as one of the most violent men in America. He was Ultra Right Wing and belonged to several hate groups including the Ku Klux Klan and the White Citizen's Council of Atlanta. He told an informant of the pending assassination and was both photographed and filmed on the eastern curb of Houston Street across from Dealey Plaza and out of range of any stray bullet on 22 November 1963. He died on 9 February 1974 two weeks after a Coleman stove blew up in his Georgia mansion. The mortician who prepared his body for burial felt that the wounds would not have been severe enough to cause his death.

CF - Page 562
HT - Page 475

Q. Dave Yaras?

A. He was a close friend of both Jack Ruby and Jimmy Hoffa and was the prime suspect in several gangland slayings. He was murdered in 1974.

C - Page 494
CF - Page 563
DC - Page 329

Q. Clay Shaw?

A. He was the director of the International Trade Mart in New Orleans with reported ties to the CIA and David Ferrie. He was the only person brought to trial for conspiracy in the death of President Kennedy, but was acquitted. A neighbor of Shaw saw an ambulance pull up in front of Shaw's house in the French Quarter of New Orleans on 14 August 1974. The neighbor saw two men carrying a sheet-covered body on a stretcher into the house. The men left quickly and Shaw was reportedly "found dead in his home alone" several hours later. The cause of death on the death certificate signed by Dr. Hugh Betson was lung cancer but other sources say that his body was embalmed before being examined by the coroner to determine the cause of death.

CF - Page 563
HT - Page 144
OTT - Page 274

Q. Roscoe White?

A. He was the self-professed gunman on the Grassy Knoll who claimed that he fired the fatal head shot and that he killed 28 witnesses. He died of injuries sustained in an explosive fire in 1971. He admitted his involvement in the assassination before he died.

Austin American-Statesman August 5 & 7 1990
DC - Page

Q. Earle Cabell?

A. He was Mayor of Dallas at the time of the assassination. He later became a U.S. Representative from Texas. He died of natural causes in 1974.

CF - Page 563

Q. Sam Giancana?

A. He was a Chicago Mafia boss who reportedly told his brother that he had sent "Chuckie" Nicoletti, "Milwaukee Phil" Alderisio and Richard Cain to Dallas and that they had been the shooters in the Texas School Book Depository. He

was killed with a .22 caliber pistol on 19 June 1975 shortly
before he was due to testify before the Senate Intelligence
Committee. According to authors Groden and Livingstone
that type of weapon would not be used by a mob killer but
rather someone with "intelligence" connections.

C - Page 494
CF - Page 563
DC - Page 2
HT - Page 141

Q. Clyde Tolson?

A. He was Hoover's assistant and "living mate" who reportedly helped Hoover's secretary destroy files after Hoover's
death. Tolson had open-heart surgery in the summer of 1963.
He died of "natural causes" in 1975.

CF - Page 563
HT - Page 68

Q. Allan Sweatt?

A. He was the Chief Criminal Deputy Sheriff in Dallas involved with the assassination investigation. He reportedly

was given an assassination photograph taken by Mary Moorman. The photograph later disappeared. He died in July 1975 of "natural causes".

CF - Page 563
HT - Page 123

Q. General Earl Wheeler?

A. He was the contact between the CIA and President Kennedy. He died of "unknown causes" in December 1975.

CF - Page 563

Q. James Chaney?

A. He was a Dallas motorcycle officer who was riding behind and to the right of President Kennedy. He said the President had been "struck in the face" by a bullet. He died in April 1976 reportedly of a "heart attack".

CF - Page 563
HT - Page 232

Q. Dr. Charles Gregory?

A. He was one of Governor Connally's physicians who stated that the bullet which hit him "behaved as though it had never struck anything except him". He also died in April 1976, reportedly of a "heart attack".

CF - Page 563
HT - Page 64

Q. William Harvey?

A. He reportedly coordinated the CIA-Mafia plots against Castro for the CIA. He died in June 1976 of "complications following heart surgery".

CF - Page 563
HT - Page 312

Q. Johnny Roselli?

A. He was an underworld figure with involvement in the CIA-Mafia assassination plots against Castro. He testified once before the Senate Assassinations Committee and was due to appear again. His body was found in a metal drum floating in Dumfoundling Bay near North Miami Beach, Florida in July 1976. He had been suffocated, stabbed and dismembered.

C - Page 496
CF - Page 563
FH - Page 415
HT - Page 141

Q. William Pawley?

A. He was the former ambassador to Brazil with connections to organized crime figures and anti-Castro Cubans. He died from a gunshot wound in January 1977. His death was ruled a "suicide".

C - Page 498
CF - Page 565
HT - Page 145

Q. George DeMohrenschildt?

A. One of Oswald's closest friends in Dallas, De-Mohrenschildt was a White Russian count with a background in intelligence. He died of a gunshot wound within hours of being located by an investigator for the Assassinations Committee. His death, too, was ruled a "suicide".

C - Page 492
CF - Page 565
DC - Page 356
HT - Page 189

Q. Carlos Prio Soccaras?

A. He was a former president of Cuba and raised money for anti-Castro Cubans. He was shot and killed one week after George DeMohrenschildt died. His death was ruled a "suicide".

C - Page 492
CF - Page 565
HT - Page 145

Q. Lou Staples?

302

A. He was the host of a Dallas radio show who told friends of his plan to "break the assassination case". He died of a gunshot wound to the head in May 1977. It was ruled a "suicide".

CF - Page 565

Q. Louis Nichols?

A. He was J. Edgar Hoover's special assistant and his liaison with the Warren Commission while working on the assassination investigation. He died of a "heart attack" in June 1977, the first of six top FBI officials to die that year. All six had been scheduled to testify before the House Select Committee on Assassinations.

CF - Page 565

Q. Alan Belmont?

A. He also was a special assistant to J. Edgar Hoover and testified before the Warren Commission. He died after a "long illness" in August 1977.

CF - Page 565

Q. James Cadigan?

A. He was a document expert for the FBI and had access to classified assassination documents. He died as the result of a fall in his home in August 1977.

CF - Page 565

Q. Joseph Ayres?

A. He was President Kennedy's Chief stewart aboard *Air Force One*. He was killed in a "shooting accident" in August 1977.

CF - Page 565

Q. Francis Gary Powers?

A. He piloted a U-2 spy plane which was shot down over Russia during the time Oswald was living there. He expressed the opinion that Oswald may have given the Russians the information needed to down his plane. He died in a helicopter crash in August 1977. Reportedly he "ran out of fuel".

CF - Page 565

Q. Kenneth O'Donnell?

A. He was a close friend and aide to President Kennedy who said he heard two shots from the Grassy Knoll. He died of "natural causes" in September 1977.

CF - Page 565

Q. Donald Kaylor?

A. He was a fingerprint expert for the FBI and examined prints found at the scene of the assassination. He died of an apparent heart attack in October 1977.

CF - Page 565

Q. J.M. English?

A. He was the head of the FBI laboratory where Oswald's alleged pistol and rifle were tested. He, too, died of an apparent heart attack in October 1977.

CF - Page 565

Q. William Sullivan?

A. He was the former number three man with the FBI whose testimony was sought by the House Select Committee on Assassinations. He was shot and killed in November 1977 by a man who claimed he had "mistaken him for a deer". The "hunter" was charged with a misdemeanor and released to the custody of his father, a New Hampshire state policeman. No further investigation of Sullivan's death was conducted.

C - Page 497
CF - Page 565
HT - Page 145

Q. C.L. "Lummie" Lewis?

A. He was the Dallas deputy sheriff who arrested Mafia-connected Jim Braden in Dealey Plaza following the assassination. He died of "natural causes" in 1978.

CF - Page 565

Q. Jesse Curry?

A. He was the Dallas Chief of Police at the time of the assassination. He reportedly died of a "heart attack" in June 1980.

CF - Page 566

Q. Dr. John Holbrook?

A. He was the psychiatrist who said that Ruby was sane. His cause of death in June 1980 was ruled due to a heart attack, but notes and pills were found at the scene.

CF - Page 566

Q. Marguerite Oswald?

A. She was Lee's mother. Until her death of cancer in January 1981 she maintained that her son had worked for the government and that he was innocent of involvement in the assassination.

CF - Page 566

Q. Dr. James Weston?

A. He was a pathologist who was allowed to see the JFK autopsy material for the House Select Committee on Assassinations. He died while jogging in May 1982, it was ruled due to "natural causes".

CF - Page 566

Q. Will H. Griffin?

A. He was the FBI agent who reportedly identified Oswald as "definitely" being an informant for the FBI. He died of "cancer" in August 1982.

CF - Page 566

Q. W. Marvin Gheesling?

A. He was an FBI official who assisted in supervising the investigation of JFK's death. He reportedly died of "natural causes" in October 1982.

CF - Page 566

Q. Roy Kellerman?

A. He was the Secret Service agent-in-charge of President Kennedy's limousine on 22 November 1963. He rode in the front seat with the driver, William Greer. He died of unknown causes in March 1984.

CF - Page 566
HT - Page 148

Epilogue

I was fourteen years old when President Kennedy died. I remember exactly where I was, and exactly how I felt when I heard about the assassination. My initial feeling was disbelief, quickly followed by fear. How could this have happened, and what will happen to us now? He was trying to make the world a better place and then he was gone. The loss was felt around the world and nothing has been the same since. We will never know how different our lives might have been if he had lived.

JHB

Q. How did the rest of the world react to the assassination?

A. We are told Westminster Abbey's bell in London tolled for one hour. Every store in Paris closed. The Vienna Opera was cancelled. In Ireland all radio programs were cancelled and in Berlin 300,000 people marched by torchlight.

HT - Page 463

The Final Question

Q. How did President Kennedy want to be remembered?

A. He said "All I want them to say about me is what they said about John Adams, 'He kept the peace'." In the speech he was to deliver at the Dallas Trade Mart on 22 November 1963, he had planned to say: "We ask that we may be worthy of our power and responsibility, that we may exercise our strength with wisdom and restraint, and that we may achieve in our time and for all time the ancient vision of 'peace on earth, goodwill toward men'".

PA - Page 303

Photo Credits: Richard Hart, p.129 top; Douglass H. Hubbard, p.129 bottom; Henry Yardum, p.170 top; author, p.156 bottom, p.157 top, p.163 bottom, p.167 top left & right, p.169 top left & right, p.172 bottom, left & right, p.173 top, left & right, p.174 top, p.175 top, left & right, p.192, all other photos courtesy of the JFK Assassination Information Center and thanks to all the photographers involved.

For further assassination information contact: The JFK Assassination Information Center, 603 Munger #310, Box 40, Dallas, TX 75202 or the JFK Assassination Exhibit & Research Center, 5685 Falls Ave., Niagara Falls, Ontario, Canada L2E6W7.

Staff of the JFK Assassination Information Center left to right: Robert T. Johnson, Administrator, Larry N. Howard, President & Director, Amy Thompson, Public Relations Manager, John Nagel, Director of Catalog Sales. Not shown: Coke Buchanan, Director of Communications and Larry Ray Harris, Director of Research.

Bibliography

Act of Treason by Mark North, Carroll & Graf Publishers, Inc., New York, N.Y., 1991

Best Evidence by David Lifton , Carroll & Graf Publishers, Inc., New York, N.Y., 1988

Conspiracy by Anthony Summers, Paragon House, New York, N.Y., 1989

Contract on America by David Scheim, Kensington Publishing Corp., New York, N.Y., 1988

Crossfire by Jim Marrs, Carroll & Graf Publishers, Inc., New York, N.Y., 1989

Death Of A President by William Manchester, Harper & Row Publishers, Inc., New York , 1967

Double Cross by Sam & Chuck Giancana, Warner Books, Inc., New York, N.Y., 1992

Fatal Hour by G. Robert Blakey & Richard N. Billings, Berkley Books, New York, N.Y., 1992

High Treason by Robert Groden & Harrison Livingstone, The Berkley Publishing Group, New York, N.Y., 1990

High Treason 2 by Harrison Livingstone, Carroll & Graf Publishers, Inc. New York, N.Y., 1992

The Kennedys, An American Drama by Peter Collier & David Horowitz, Warner Books Inc., New York, N.Y, 1984

Mafia Kingfish by John Davis, NAL Penguin, Inc., New York, N.Y., 1989

On The Trail Of The Assassins by Jim Garrison, Sheridan Square Press, New York, N.Y., 1988

Peter Lawford, The Man Who Kept The Secrets by James

Spada, Bantam Books, New York, N.Y., 1991

Presidential Anecdotes by Paul F. Boller, Jr., Penguin Books, USA Inc., New York, N.Y., 1982

Plausible Denial by Mark Lane, Thunder's Mouth Press, New York, N.Y., 1991

Presidential Passions by Michael Sullivan, Shapolsky Publishers, Inc., New York, N.Y., 1991

The Ruby Cover-up by Seth Kantor, Zebra Books, Kensingtron Publishing Company, New York, N.Y., 1992

Reasonable Doubt by Henry Hurt, Henry Holt & Company, Inc., New York, N.Y., 1985

Rush to Judgement by Mark Lane, Thunder's Mouth Press, New York N.Y., 1992

Spy Saga by Philip H. Melanson, Praeger Publishers, New York, N.Y., 1990

The Texas Connection by Craig I. Zirbel, The Texas Connection Company, Scottsdale, Arizona, 1991

INDEX